HUNGRY WOMEN

Hungry Women

Nina Mozee

Library of Congress Control Number:		2011900602
ISBN:	Hardcover	978-1-4568-4843-9
	Softcover	978-1-4568-4842-2
	Ebook	978-1-4568-4844-6

This book was printed in the United States of America.

To order additional copies of this book, contact:
Xlibris Corporation
1-888-795-4274
www.Xlibris.com
Orders@Xlibris.com
90298

CONTENTS

Preface 11
Acknowledgments 13

Part I

Whatever 21
Good Couch! Bad Couch! 24
Gettin' Right 26
I'm Hooked 28
What About Me 31
A Snake's-Eye View 33
Mo' Love! Mo' Better! 36
Getting Strong and Looking Back 38
All for Nothing 44
Shame 46
My Womb! My Womb! 49
My Girl 50
Green Is Good 51
Out of Order 52
Run 53
We Got It 54
Step It Up 56
Stuck Like Glue 59
Click 62
Traveling Light 64
My Dreams, My Thoughts 66
Red Rooster 68
The Champ Is Coming, The Champ Is Coming 70
Tea Time 72
Heck, No! 73
The Mess! 74
Smart or Dumb? (Choose One!) 75

Stick to the Rules 77
That's the Break's 78
Lies, Lies, No-ho More Lies 80
Gossip 82
Your Treasures 84
Hungry 89

Part II

Dancing 95
Out of the Tunnel 98
Work Harder 100
In This Generation 103
Nurses Are Good 106
Doctors Are Special 108
Let the Good Times Roll 110
It's Your Day 114
Misery, Why Do You Love Company? 116
Let's Be Thankful 119
Forever Mother and Daughter 121
Hidden Talents 123
Play On 125
Pass It On 127
True You 130
Corn 132
Nibble and Devour 134
Hidden Camera 136
Resolved 138

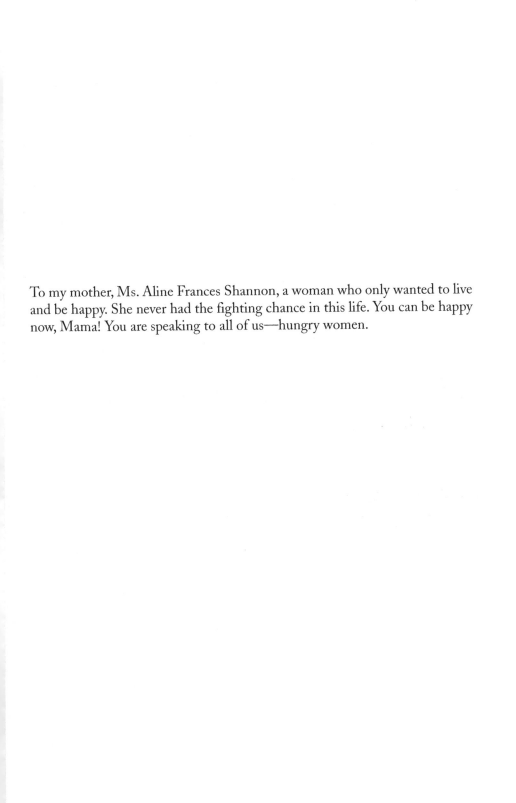

To my mother, Ms. Aline Frances Shannon, a woman who only wanted to live and be happy. She never had the fighting chance in this life. You can be happy now, Mama! You are speaking to all of us—hungry women.

MUST GO FORWARD

God gave the spirit of harvest, and some of that spirit was sprinkled on me as a young girl sitting on the back steps of my little yard. I heard my desires; I saw my dreams even in the fear of the surroundings I grew up in!

So I humbly wish to put this manuscript in the hands and minds of our lovely growing society and certainly mature women of our today.

Lean In Here!

Ladies and gentlemen, to know our "choice is our destiny."

Congratulations!

Holding this book in your hands, you are making a better choice to head forward to achieve all your challenging goals in this life.

Slam fear out of your way! Get inspired to stand boldly! This book will unveil a true story. My concern is we must know and understand things and people.

Preface

I pray our hearts will meet in this book and agree on what we must do to make it right!

Hungry women, it's time to start cookin' with togetherness, style, and love!

Acknowledgments

Let me give my first recognition to my savior and my lord, my king, my heartbeat of every minute, every second of my life, my love, Jesus Christ!

We bow to the King of kings!

For we, three sisters, never knew how we were kept from harm and danger. We came up holding and trying to protect one another. All the time we were holding on to one another. We were really holding on to him, our Father who art in heaven! Thinking and being determined of not ever letting go of each other, we know now we could not let go of his unchanging hand, which always kept us together in the first place. Even though we did not realize it, this is the most beautiful part of holding on . . . Now we know why!

I want to thank my lord and savior Jesus Christ for inspiring me to tell my story; my two older sisters—Shirley Daniels a.k.a. Cissy and Donna Polk—for always loving me. They have always been there for me through thick and thin. Thanks to my three children, Katrina, Vincent Jr., and Jermaine, for listening and believing and standing at my back as the soldiers that you are; Jermaine, for being so sweet and understanding through the years, you always love your Mama no matter what, thank you baby—you're cute. I miss you much. To Vincent Jr., my Vinny, my Billydee, you push Mama when I needed to push on, no matter what the task, you are every mother's dream (believe that)! I thank you my oldest son, (Mama loves you). And I thank you my daughter Katrina for being so concern and forgiving when I fall short, you always step in and give me the word I need to carry on and thank you Trina for your laughter, I always loved it, you just be steadfast and keep your joy because that brings me through (Mama loves her). To my pastor Paul Burleson and his wife, Evangelist Dallas Burleson, for your wisdom, teaching, and love. To all my nieces and nephews, for being who you are in my life, and most of all, to my Ky-Ky for having my back. A special thanks to Mr. Mozee. To my brothers-in-law that I love dearly, thank you for taking good care of my sisters and me. To the girls, my crew, you know who you are, and I love you all dearly; thank you for being with me through the years. Special thanks to my girl Jackie, you left me too soon, but I ain't mad. R.I.P. Last of all, thank you Morris Cummings for helping me direct my life at a young age.

PART I

To all my girls, you are my sisters. To every sister on God's earth, black, yellow, white, green, or purple, we are sisters. Like it or not, you are my sister! We all have red blood in our veins. We eat, sleep, and drink, don't we? Because of our sisterhood, we must get together in this book. Our first bond is in this book together, and we will come out of this book together. In this book, this tunnel, where we share our spirits, our thoughts, our hearts, we must communicate like we never have in our lives. We are getting along with age, a lot of us, and don't have time to wait, put off, or pretend anymore. We have already wasted enough time.

Usually when things are right and in order, we want people to sometimes say that! It's not asking too much, ladies, to get our pat on the back every now and then. If we had a helping hand in something good and positive, take your bow. Yes, take your bow for what you've done to make the world a better place. This is the place we have until God calls us. We all know the world would not be what it is unless we put our thumb in the pie. That's why God made woman special, believe me! WE ARE SPECIAL! We must think of ourselves as the most special person we have ever looked at. The enemy will tell us that we are nothing, and we don't know anything. He will come at us through our loved ones, so watch that so you will know how to handle the situation.

When it comes, and it will come, he will never stop causing problems. That's what he does; that's all he does day and night. And that's why, ladies, God tells us over and over to put on the whole armor for war. If you don't know what your armor is, please open your Bible because you and I must learn how to fight this war. It starts with a holy war, and that's why the enemy tries to fool us into thinking the war is within us, within your family member, within your loved one, within your job, but the war is really within the enemy. That's why he's so unhappy, especially when we're happy. So stay alert, and keep your eye on the sparrow. So girls look out, and look up the word *WOMAN*.

W = Wisdom you'll have and must use.

O = Opportunity is there if you open your eyes.

M = Motherhood. We have to guide our children to the right way.

A = Awesome is the way we can bear pain to bring forth another life.

N = Noble are the minds that make a way no matter what while holding up the household with love, peace, and happiness. Ladies, you're so special.

All of us are needed more than we will ever know. That's why it's important for us to stay together, mentally and physically, and as ladies. We are fighting the same war here on earth. We will say with pride: I am somebody because God doesn't make no junk! And we must believe that; if we don't, who will? Well, as long as we know who we are, then ladies we are on our way to the straight and narrow. I don't care if we are in school or out of school, fat or skinny, up or down, keep looking up. Good things are in our paths because we have that brick wall up, and nothing ugly or bad can break the love down. Now let's talk about STINKIN' THINKIN'!

Ladies, we are all about the word *woman* and more; oh, why do we think less of ourselves? Do we blame it on others, or is it the woman in the mirror? Is she in the mirror? A lot of us can answer that question in a million different ways. But listen, she can change, she can be corrected. The way I answer that question is, blame it all on our foolish, foolish decisions and choices we make. Start taking your time, relax, and think, ladies; we don't have to be in a hurry. BREATH. We truly have wisdom, opportunity, motherhood, awesomeness, and the noble mind of our god. We just don't use it all the time; for some of us, never! Why don't we care and stop and ask ourselves, is this a wise choice for me and my children? Yes, ladies, a lot of us take our children through hell because of our choices; you know, we do.

That's not fair to them. I say, forgive me, children, for my silly, dumb choices; Mom is so sorry! Ladies, we don't check our choices out first; instead, we jump into the pool with only a little water in it, telling yourself, "I can get in the pool full of water later. Right now, I need to get wet." It's all right, ladies, to think about yourself and your wants, your desires, but why let them be low desires and low wants? We have to be the one that demands the classy wants and high-standard desires. We will shine like glitter girls with the high-standard desires. And all will see God in us; you can't say you belong to God then walk around looking like you don't know what a comb and brush is. We have to keep ourselves looking clean and godly; God is a clean god. And there is a song that says, "I want to be more like him." Well, if we're like him, we're clean inside and out. We don't walk around in public with our hair out of order. We want others to see God in us when our hair is in order.

We represent God; well, YOUR HAIR IS YOUR GLORY, so let's watch that appearance, ladies. (Isn't this good!) The way we get to low choices is through low thinking. Well, I'll say low STINKIN' THINKIN', ladies. When we think like that, there is a question, where did I get those kinds of thoughts from? Did I listen to someone? Did I read that somewhere? Is this my inheritance? Maybe a curse! Oh, it's got to be from the code, DNA. No, no, no, girls ! It's a cop out! We won't say to ourselves, "I DON'T THINK LIKE THAT. IT'S NOT ME!" We just look in the mirror and say, "WHATEVER!"

WHATEVER

Ladies, we are stronger than that. If you don't think you are, then you would not even be wasting your time reading this book. But you are destined to read this book because when you finish it, you will truly know that today is the first day of the rest of your life, and you will be very sure of where you're going; and now, ladies, you can know why. And you will say, "Yes, I've got to make each day count! I have no time to lose." You're going up, up, up with love. Ladies, you've had it all the time. For you, it's up with prayers, up with your confidence then look at yourself in the mirror, and know and see how good you look. This great feeling, means up with something, will make you want to buy for you (some smell-good perfume and those glamorous pair of shoes), you know, all the ways and means to make you happy.

It comes with love, not the word *WHATEVER*! LADIES, LADIES, now guess what, *WHATEVER* gets us. *WHATEVER* gets us to cover up instead of dressed because all eyes are on me! *WHATEVER* gets us minimum-wage jobs instead of top-dollar, money-making jobs. *WHATEVER* gets our children nothing but a wish list out in the world and at home. *WHATEVER* gets us on the bus instead of in our "NEW CAR" in the driveway. Lastly, *WHATEVER* gets us a sorry, sorry, no caring, NO having nothing, can't ever get nothing, don't know nothing, wanting six or seven women to buy him something, germ-spreading, not ever going to be nothing, sleeping in the backyard under the raincoat, no-TV-having, wish he had a watch on his wrist, not ever going to get a job or a car, cigarette-begging, need a bath and can't take one, looking and licking in the Dumpster, following homeless women around, pitiful, poor excuse of a man.

That's what *WHATEVER* gets us, ladies, so please be very careful how you use that word. Try not to put that word in your vocabulary at all. That way, it won't show up in your lives. HEY, GIRLS, you know, I think I should have been a judge! I really think I would have been a good one, to help put lives back together again. "HUMPTY DUMPTY" if you will! YOU THINK? I know as I got older, I started getting more knowledge about different things in the world. This word *FOUNDATION* caught my attention. I remember hearing adults using that word quite a bit, so I had to pay attention to that word, and as I grew up, I wanted to investigate it. I needed to find out why I never had a foundation! And if I had one, why didn't I pay attention so I could keep the foundation? Now, ladies, this word was of good status, and everyone loved having a foundation. I just didn't know the bread was there, so I didn't bite! The boots were there, girls. I just didn't put them on, with my silly self. And I should have, my life would have been so much better now that I can SEE! I made bad choices, ladies. I didn't make it count!

Now I've lost that phase of my life and can't get it back. And I want to so bad. I can't get it back, ladies, don't you see and hear me? Are you or were you on this side of the fence? Are you thinking of pancakes only? Why can't we say we don't have time for guys right now! How are we going to make a guy happy when we can't make ourselves happy?

Don't you know, a real man, a serious man, wants a serious woman that makes good choices, smart choices about her money, being there and taking care of her children on a top-notch level, shopping smart, and dressing herself smart. If you have children that aren't his, he is watching how you take care of the one you have 'cause a good mother usually makes good wife material, and a smart man knows that! We need to keep ourselves at an unavailable status most of the time than when he is in our presence; he will treasure the moment. We must keep ourselves special. Ladies, once we let that guard down, we will be treated just as plain as a slice of bread.

If he's a player, then you have to carry yourself as a queen; you can't let him forget you came from a high calling. Girls, we have to hold up the female banner. He usually won't marry you if he can sleep with you without a commitment. Ladies, we can't go low in the valley; there's no one that cares about you down there, so we have to stay on top of the mountain where our pride is. The ladies that are hard to get are the ones they want. Pastor Paul Burleson says, "Why buy the cow when the milk is free!" So we have to really think about that! Stop being so hard up for a male in your life, they aren't going anywhere. What GOD has for you is really for you. A lot of us say or think, GOD is too slow and we are in a hurry, and that's how we end up with the crumbs. MEN, SEX, AND NIGHTCLUBS will be here until Jesus comes; they aren't going anywhere, so what's the big RUSH? Use your youth to prepare for the real man God has for you to spend the rest of your life with. Let GOD get the bride ready. If you're in his bed, GOD cannot get the bride ready. Ladies, please, make each day count; if you're anywhere near making a choice in this part of your life, think about the POWER of making the "RIGHT" choice and the power of making the wrong choice! We have to think, ladies. DO IT FOR YOURSELF. HEY! DO IT FOR ME TOO! We're in this together, you know! LET'S DO THIS!

Good Couch! Bad Couch!

- Ladies, as I look back I had such an everyday life. As a child, I was always over other friend's houses—eating, playing, watching TV, or spending the night. Because my little house we called home was a "whatever!" home, whatever you needed was not there. I found it at one of my friend's houses. Oh yes, I found food, TV, fun, and love at someone else's house. Since I knew that I had that problem as a child, why did I not make sure I made better choices as a woman? There is a little joke about that: will you choose the bad couch or the good couch? Ladies, would you choose the good couch with fluffy pillows and soft cushions that smell like roses and powder or the bad couch with smelly sourness, like stinky feet, with wires sticking out to hurt you? Now who in their right mind would choose that bad couch? When you can see it, smell it, why take a chance and sit there? We can't fix it. The wires are out of it. We see that!

- The good couch is right there, so why is the bad couch so damn crowded? What, ladies? What? Do we not like soft couches with fluffy pillows? Why do so many of us choose to sit on that nasty, ugly couch? Our choices are our DESTINY, and DESTINY is forever. I can't sit on that nasty couch forever; it's uncomfortable. Do you feel that on your butt? It hurts! We can't, we can't stay there forever; how are we going to get up? We know where God put us when we first got here on earth. And we seem to have lost our way. THOUGH falling down is not a bad thing, the bad thing is not getting up! Ladies, we can get up; we have to help each other get up and stay up. Listen up, girls. We have to want to get up. QUESTION: Why is there so many of us that don't want to get up? WHO CAN FIND A VIRTUOUS WOMAN? HER PRICE IS FAR BEYOND RUBIES!

What is your price? Can you hear God saying, your price for getting up will cost you NOTHING! Jesus paid for it all. Our getting up is paid for, ladies. So take his hand and get up. That's the way we do it; this is the only way we can do it. Now, haven't we tried everything else that just drops us right back down? Sometimes deeper than where we were. Ladies, I'm tired of it, aren't you? We have to make better things happen for us. Girls, we have to step up, step out, and step together, encourage one another, praying for one another through the tunnels. And, ladies, we have got to be truthful and be real, no more pretending. God knows when we pretend, and we can't get through the tunnel pretending. So stop it! It doesn't work, okay!

Ladies, we have the knack to always give into the negative situations. I once had a real good friend; she was in grade school with me, but now she has passed on. But I sure remember her making a choice of taking a drug called chocolate chip. And the guy next door started looking real, real cute to her. So she invited him in, and he ended up spending the night with her. The next day, she woke up and saw all the big-lipped monster's true looks, and she screamed. Oh Jesus! What have I done? She was praying and hoping she did not make a baby.

That night, she knew she made a bad choice; first of all, for taking the chocolate chip drug, which led her into thinking she liked being with the guy next door. And it could have been a lot more of a problem to deal with the rest of her life that God gave her here. We take too many chances, ladies. We have to watch that we end up in places we can't remember how we got there, just so glad to wake up. You know what? Some women are found and can't and don't ever wake up.

So just keeping you on your toes, ladies. We must make better choices for ourselves. Back in the days when I was in high school, girls would stick together with letting one another slip off with a boy alone or get into his car alone. It used to be, "you ride one, you ride all." But now, in this day and time, it's so popular to be alone in a car with a guy, but we all know, ladies. It's still dangerous. Even more than ever. Why do we take such chances on men and won't take any kind of chance to get in the car and ride with Jesus? He's our main man anyway; he loves us, keeps us, takes care of us, provides for us, opens doors for us, protects us. So what's up with that, ladies? Can't we think and make wise decisions? Well, we are in another year now. I feel good about that part of making a new start, getting another chance of making things better, getting me right.

Gettin' Right

Getting me right! What does that really mean to you and me? FACT: I got my man; I have a good man. He works, makes good money, pays the bills, talks to me pretty decent, dresses well (looks good in his clothes too!), doesn't have a filthy mouth. He came from a pretty good background, well, a broken home, but all in all, raised well. Has good morals, makes me love him sometime. I don't have to work, and I have a maid who comes in twice a week. So I stay in the beauty shops, have to get those nails and feet done! You know, I love me; I'm what I call high maintenance. Things have to be right since I'm getting me right; yes, I'm all right on the outside. You know what my maintenance looks like on the inside?

THE INSIDE: HE MAKES ME SICK! Just because he works and makes the money, he thinks I should always cook a hot meal, humph! I need him to take me out to eat. Is he crazy? I can't stand over a hot stove. My back hurts; my legs get tired.

Yes, getting right! Fix him lunch. Oh! I'm getting right. He better stop and get himself some fast foods to eat; why do you think they have fast foods for? Whatever! Then he wants his clothes washed, take the kids and make sure they eat and have clean clothes, make sure they do their homework for school. Is he saying I don't do anything around here? Why is he finding something to keep me busy, huh? I don't think so! He better get him some business, maybe he got me twisted!

Then he wants to pray all the time. I love God, but I don't need to pray when he says so. Who does he think he is? He's not perfect; it's not me that needs to pray anyway. Well, ARE THOSE THOUGHTS GETTING US RIGHT, ladies? Sister, don't you know when you've got it good, girl? And, girl, you better recognize. Some other women would love a man like that—with money, has a maid, and giving you makeup! That's the life, isn't it! First of all, ladies, why are we not thankful? Some of us know we don't deserve that good treatment that a lot of us have, and when God blesses us with such happiness, WE ARE MAD! Oh! But we love God, remember? HE KNOWS MY HEART! Yes, he knows our hearts, ladies, so we better be a little more thoughtful to our mates if God sent a good one down your path. God SAID, "A WISE WOMAN BUILDS HER HOUSE UP, AND A FOOLISH WOMAN TEARS IT DOWN." Now, ladies, a wise woman will build her house up. Building your house up does not always mean decorating it. Get this, ladies, God meant to build our house up with love, understanding, care, trust, wanting, giving, needing, sharing, prayer, song, and being who you need to be when you need to be who you are.

To do this, ladies, the way God says it, we have to have the wisdom, knowledge, and most of all, understanding. Now, when a foolish woman tears her house down, it's usually torn down and, most of the time, will be very hard to build back up without the wisdom, knowledge, and understanding. And the love surely has to be there to build it back up. A foolish woman tears her house down with hurtful words, uncaring, no emotions, no presentation, no imagination, lots of pride, and lack of understanding because if you don't understand what you're doing there in that home, well then, you shouldn't be there anyway because you don't know what you're doing. That's why you're tearing it down.

God said, "If man has an ear, let him hear!" Well, ladies, you have ears also, so listen when someone is giving you wisdom. An older woman will usually have wisdom to give you because they've been there and done that. Usually, she can tell you how to go around the flame so you won't get burned. But when you're silly, stubborn, and won't listen to anyone, your house will be torn down. Ladies, you set the atmosphere in your home; that's why God says, "You build it up, or you will tear it down." You dot all the *i*'s in your home. You make happiness or you make sadness or you're just plain mean. Take your pick! And if you don't know why you're the way you are and you're not trying to find out that you need a wake-up call, RING, RING, RING.

I'M HOOKED

LADIES, listen up! I've learned that the word *hooked* is related to the words *addicted, habituated, buttoned, cuff-linked, zippered, buckled*, and *snapped*. So if you look at the words and picture in your mind each word, you can see and know they are connected or gripped, if you will, to something or someone and keeping something together or shut in. And all these words take the position of *hooked*. Now being hooked, snapped, and buttoned can seem to be a thought of safety or being safe, but *addicted* or *habituated* don't seem safe to me. But they go with that word *hooked*, and most of the time, when you see the word *hooked* or hear the word *hooked*, it means something very ugly and permanent. Something most people don't want to talk about. And we, women, well, when were hooked, it's usually to something or someone we need and should be away from. Ladies, I need your attention so I can tell you about my life of being hooked and unhooked to all the right and wrong things. I recall a time in my life when I was living in California. I was invited to go on this guy's yacht, and I was with some pretty nice trusting people that were well-to-do financially, so I accepted the invitation. And I got dressed real cute; I surely had my weight down real nice back then, ladies! And I was ready to go on a boat ride. I had never been on such a boat ride in my life, so I was happy about being able to go. So we got there on the pier and then got on the yacht! It was so pretty inside; it had orange carpet all over and a built-in bed, a nice wet bar and cabinets, and a table and a booth that you sit in to eat. It was just real pretty, so I sat down in the booth with the table in front of it and propped my arm on the side border that had carpet on the armrest there. So I put my arm up there as I sat down, and my hand went down on there at the same time. AND before I could BLINK, I was YELLING and CRYING, "A FISHHOOK" that was in the carpet there; IT WENT INTO MY BABY FINGER as I sat down! I MEAN THE FISHHOOK WAS ALL THE WAY THROUGH THE TOP OF MY LITTLE FINGER! All hell broke loose, everyone was yelling out their ideas on how to get it out! (AND I WAS IN TOTAL PAIN!) And they were spending so much time trying to figure out how to get me out or get the hook out of my finger without putting me in more PAIN. Thereafter, about forty minutes or so, the owner of the yacht came in with a big knife, and he begin to cut on the orange carpet that was made on to the armrest where my finger was. And he cut a big square piece, and I WAS FREE! I came out of the booth where I was sitting, so they took me off the boat; I was still CRYING. About three or four guys had me, and one of them turned my head and two held on to me and the other one PULLED THAT FISHHOOK OUT OF MY FINGER as quickly as he could. I screamed, and my legs got weak at the same time, and I went all the way down; my legs just gave out! But they caught me before I hit the ground, and the *HOOK was out of ME FOREVER*, I THOUGHT! And I heard a man who was just looking on say, "MAN, THAT WAS A GOOD CATCH!" I didn't know at that time what he meant, but as I got older, I kinda knew what he meant. I know that we, as women, can be hooked on things way worse than that hook that had me that night. We can be hooked on things such as being HOOKED ON DOPE, HOOKED ON SEX, HOOKED ON LIQUOR, HOOKED ON SWEETS, HOOKED ON GOSSIP, HOOKED ON PIMPS, HOOKED ON BEING HOMELESS, HOOKED ON BEING JUST PLAIN DUMB, HOOKED ON NOT BATHING, HOOKED ON BEING IN JAIL, AND JUST HOOKED ON NOT THINKING AT ALL. AND THERE ARE SO MANY MORE HOOK-ONS THAT HAVE NOT BEEN MENTIONED. That fishhook was only one of the small things in this life to be hooked on to! Ladies, there are so many more ugly hooks in this world that we have to look out for and know that they mean danger FOR US! Ladies, we want and have to be hooked on to the good and the right hooks in our lives—HOOKED TO our visions, our minds that lead us to a good foundation in life; hooked to a good solid church home; hooked to the good kind of man we are proud to bring home, the kind of man that says he loves us and is willing to work and keep the bills paid so that we never have to worry about what's not paid and he will do anything to make us safe and happy; hooked to a real good job; hooked on to what our children's future will look like and what town they will call home. What town will I call home? Because if I were hooked on the right thoughts, I don't think I would have left home. I remember I was really hooked on music and singing, but I, not being hooked on being focused, was looking for love in all the wrong places. So that hook in my finger let me know that I was not hooked on anything good. BUT now, ladies, I'm hooked on GOD, and I know now he's hooked on to me. I'm hooked on to peace. I'm hooked on to my children's dreams and thoughts and their ideas. I'm hooked on to my grandsons playing sports; I'm hooked on to presenting GOD'S word and warnings on live stage. I'm hooked on to the battlefield for our lord and savior. I'm hooked on wanting to be about my father's business. I'm hooked on to knowing only what I do for Christ will last. I'm hooked on keeping the ladies around me encouraged and letting them know we all are hooked on keeping heaven in our view. We all are now hooked on knowing that with GOD all things are possible and that "HE GAVE HIS ONLY SON" that we might live! We are hooked on knowing to stand on that solid rock called JESUS and hooked on knowing that all other grounds are sinking sand. That is why, ladies, I was destined to get hooked in that boat that night! Please understand that I was hooked to know the people and things I was around with were not real at all. I had to go through that hooked tunnel to get to his light on the end of that fishhook. AND THAT'S SO REAL!

What About Me

Solitude gives a person a lot of time to think and do a little soul-searching. In my solitude, I find myself having a moment to search my own heart. I ask myself questions like where will I go this week, and what will I do to make ME smile today? Who can I call on the phone to make them happy? Who can I make smile today besides myself? I told you earlier in the book, shopping makes ME feel wonderful! Well, ladies, when the shopping is over or the money has reached its limits, what about ME then? Looking back when I was younger, I ran away from home (a onetime thing!) because I felt no one cared for me anymore. (Now I know GOD was with me then!) Anyway I felt that way. Well, I ended up at a friend's apartment with no money, no food, and really no bed to lay my head. I met a drunken guy who wanted to beat me up for trying to take some change out of his pockets when he passed out from drinking so much liquor. I gave the change I had back and ran out the door. Then I got a ride and went over to my other girlfriend's house; her mother let me spend two nights, then I was told to go home. When I began to walk toward home, I thought to myself, *What are you doing out here walking alone? You're the one who has all the advice and jokes! And now you're all alone.* I thought, *Well, no one wants me around anymore. What did I do to feel like this? WHAT ABOUT ME?* When I got home, my father, who I hardly ever saw, put out a pickup on me. With the popo. So my sister said I should turn myself in, and we went to juvenile hall—a place for bad kids; I knew I didn't belong there. Anyway, "juve" was halfway around the corner from our house on Lafayette Street, where they booked me in. I could look out the window and see my backyard. (What punishment!) I had kitchen duty, and I was told to wash these big, big, giant "cooking pots." They were so big a human being could climb up inside of them! So they kept me about five days, all I could think of was why I was here. Did I kill somebody? Finally, I went to court, and the judge gave me one year of probation. *For running away?* OH WELL! I had to do what I was told. I remember thinking, *I'm fifteen years old, and I got myself in a mess for nothing (all for nothing).* I paid attention to that phrase. Listen up, ladies. I was not making good choices for myself, and my destiny was probation once a week at the city and county building in the juvenile department. Even in the snow, I had to catch the bus and go to report to my probation officer. Report nothing. All she said when I got there was "Take a card, we'll see you next week." I said to myself, *YOU WISH.* Then I was so angry walking back to the bus stop, and the bus was just leaving. I yelled, but it kept going. I CRIED OUT, "What about me?" Why do I feel so unloved? Well, as I started growing up, I found the answer to that question. *I was not loving myself!* And when I started loving myself, I was happier than I had ever been. My baby niece started walking when I got home from the mean place. Her name is Kyla; she missed me for those five days. She loved her auntie, and she says she still does, so I'm real happy about her saying that. Sometimes it is good to tell your aunts and uncles and grandmothers and grandfathers that you love them; they need to hear that. So I started hanging around teenagers that seem to be doing the right thing (most of the time). That's when I started getting involved in the drill team; I was in forever. My singing group was doing a lot of singing around Denver, and we were in a few competitions and shows. We were getting more phone calls than ever at that time! We were going to Texas to do a show with this band, but some of our parents said NO! We were too young to go on the road to sing. But we got to go around Denver and sang; at least they let us do that! My big sister and her husband were in charge of me, so they were the main ones to say no to the out-of-town singing. My phone started ringing more too. A lot of teens I knew started coming by, and I felt good about myself. Finally I had direction and a lot of things to do. So like the song says, I started "LIVING MY LIFE LIKE IT'S GOLDEN!" And I won't EVER STOP! "UNTIL"

A Snake's-Eye View

Ladies, stay with me on this one! I was just thinking one day on why men and women don't get along and stay in their marriage or a strong relationship or a lasting friendship. And I thought of how the BIBLE says EVE was tempted by the serpent in the garden to eat of the forbidden fruit. She did eat, then she went to ADAM and made him eat, and he did go as low as she was, and both were naked. We all know a snake is on his belly when he crawls, RIGHT? With two ugly eyes on each side of his ugly low face. Looking and crawling around, he only can see what is in his view, THAT WHICH IS LOW! So we know, LADIES, anything LOW is in the snake's view, such as a low, down man, acting, using, abusing other people; that's low and the serpent can see and tempt them to getting lower than they usually are. If we are low, ladies, we are in the view of the snake, and he will mess with our minds if we are on his ground level—LOW! That's why we can't be tempted like EVE; that snake must never see our eyes. We are never to be in a snake's-eye view; that way he can't know what we are thinking or know what we are saying or where we are going. Nothing about us can he know because we carry ourselves on a HIGH LEVEL AT ALL TIMES. I'm saying HIGH in THOUGHT, HIGH in SPEAKING, HIGH in CHARACTER, HIGH IN PRAYING. Ladies, we are so high on the mountain that snake will never get to see or hear from us ever again. WHEN our men are LOW, get away from them; they are getting ready to have a visit with the snake, which will make him want to hate and hurt you, me, us! A lot are stuck with that snake's-eye view. My point here, ladies, if men are talking, threatening, and trying to keep us low as they think, and just think deeper about this, we were the ones being tempted by the snake in the first place; he messed with us first. Eve was sorry she bit the apple but talked Adam into taking his bite; she stepped away, and Adam took over being low. We need our men to help bring us up to a good level, to be pleasing to GOD; we are sorry about Eve's lowness. HER sin made all of us be punished and cursed with labor pains while into childbirth, and we have a lot of pain because of her being in the eye view of the serpent. And we need to be able to come up to a higher ground with our men; that is why we were put here on this earth. And it's so very hard because the men that were put here for most of us are not uplifting. WHY? They are in the snake's-eye view, and he is able to tempt them. Most of our men don't have their "WHOLE ARMOR ON." A lot of our men don't know what the "WHOLE ARMOR" means and how powerful and smart they can be when they put it on; it's in the Bible, ladies, if you want to help yourselves and the head of your households. It is in Ephesians 6:10-18 WHERE GOD says to put on the whole armor of GOD so we can withstand the wiles of the devil, the serpent, and the snake! And then they still have that snake's-eye view on us. Some can't look at their daughters' right, their wives' right, or their mothers' right either, and some never will as long as they choose to be on their bellies and keep that snake's-eye view. The lower the belly crawls, the lower the man, and the weaker the woman. AND THAT'S SAD! Sisters, I don't want to be weak, been there and done that. And in this day and time, it is not smart to find ourselves weak. That is why I say over and over, we have to pull one another up and get each other through the tunnels of hardship, the tunnels of stress, and all the letdowns we process through this life; weak is not the word to have at the family dinner table. Seems like once you bring that word up, it hangs around. So from now on, we look at things from God's eye view—the look of peace, the look of love, and the look of understanding. And with that, ladies, we can look in and get our knowledge out of the window of God. It's so good to go to God's store and shop for our high steppin' shoes, with the purse to match to keep us lifted higher up so when God says "COME UP HITHER," we can, and then we also can get a dress and coat of the word so we can be ready to go out and win any battle put before us. Ladies, we must be ready at all times to fight the good fight of FAITH. Time is getting near. It's going to rain soon, and it will; we must have the umbrellas ready to go up! You get me? This is why I feel so sad that all our men are out of position and not ready to lead. We are to be on man's side (if you will), not taking the lead. And, ladies, we have had to take that place as head of the household; I just feel so sorry for all of us that had to. And the real bad part is there is so many of us. But the good part is we were able to take that spot and work with it! Now I need to say this, "I have one baby with him." "OK! He is my boyfriend," so we say. "We are so used to each other. I don't care if I have another baby with him. He won't go away if I have two of his children. And I don't want anyone else anyway. Well, he has no job right now, but he lives with me and our kids, so I'll keep it going as long as he stays here with us!" Ladies, we are taking the lead, planning the babies, planning the bills, the meals; we plan everything BUT A WEDDING! WHY? Most of the time we hear "I'm not ready yet!" And, ladies, we did all the leading and planning, so it is really our own fault that we are left holding the baby bottles, the Pampers, and the rent! That snake's-eye view has to come up and see what we see. When we see the view alone, we end up doing it all alone; then we go without, kids go without, and of course, he is surely without, and he still has that eye view of the snake. If we are not ready for battle, guess where we would end up? Ladies, don't let it happen. Stand firm 'cause we must have a diamond ring on our finger, and we must have a nice home, and we must have a car. To start with the babies, we must have this first. And if we don't demand it up front, it most likely will never happen. And we have to think about what kind of setting our children will have. What do we want our children to be when they grow up? That question is so necessary to ask ourselves, and it is up to us to think about that because we carry and have the babies. So, ladies, that word *NO* might have to be our best friend for a while. That's our trump card—NO! Ladies, start thinking differently about LIFE, LOVE, AND LIVING, OK? There's a movie called *Do the Right Thing*, and I never thought about the right thing until I started listening to my inner spirit. What I'm saying is take some quiet time and a hot bath, put a nice nightgown or pj's on, and have a cup of tea and relax; then just listen and you will see that you are stronger than you thought, and you and the "woman in the mirror" will become very, very good friends! AND THAT'S SO REAL!

Mo' Love! Mo' Better!

I just lost a dear, dear girlfriend of mine. My heart aches when I think about her not being here for me to call her or, when I hear the phone ring and I answer, hear her voice say, "HEEEEEEY!" But I've got to get it in my head and in my heart. No more talking to Pat! This is really a wake-up call for me—to know and remember, to make each day count—because you can't get it back. I'm so glad and thankful I got to bond with my girl Pat through her sickness and be there with comforting words for her to let her know she is not alone in the tunnel. We had so many good days, years, Christmases, Mother's Days, Easters, Fourth of Julys, and most of all, birthdays. That, we always look forward to while we were together raising our children or playing cards with our husbands.

She and I played cards very well together, and we would win a lot. Boy, did we love that winning part. Pat and I were known as the black version of "LUCY and ETHEL." We would always get into something, but we would always figure our way out. And then we would laugh, look at each other, and she would say, "GIRRRRL" and fall on the couch and laugh some more. We had more times laughing than anything. It's so special.

When you have a friend, a close friend, that makes you laugh most of the time. Laughing is so important, ladies. I don't know how I would have made it through without it being part of my life, without that laughter with Pat. So, Pat, I salute you for being who you were and who you are in my life. I know God put us together to encourage each other through this life. We went through good or bad, happy or sad; we were there for each other. (AND THAT'S REAL!) I know you're in heaven; I miss you much! I remember the songs you used to sing. I always love to hear you sing the gospel song "I WON'T COMPLAIN." WOOO! She surely could sing that song! Then, you had one called "NO REGRETS" by Phoebe Snow, and last of all, the song "SENDING OUT AN SOS" BY SIDE EFFECT. I was trying to get her to come to my church and sing; that didn't work out soon enough. God had other plans for Pat.

But, ladies, she was sick, what is wrong with us? And when will we come through the tunnel? We have our health and strength and can't get it together. We have to use our strength and knowledge and start speaking and acting on MO' BETTER ways and means to live this life to the fullest. When we are positive about ourselves—the way we think, drink, eat, shop, speak, and most of all, love ourselves better—then we can love others MO' BETTER; you can't and won't like or love anyone if you don't like and love yourself. Others can't love you if you don't love yourself! And if you don't have any love to give, then please, please don't look for any; it won't be there when you decide to reach for it. Ladies, we can't make it up here on this earth with no love.

Getting Strong and Looking Back

When I say no love, that is not an opening door to go to the club and get the first guy that asks you to dance or for your phone number; he does not love you. Don't look for love in all the wrong places. We have got to look for love from above first, then the love will fall on you everywhere else more than you would dream it could because God is LOVE, and until we recognize that, we will always be pretenders. Ladies, the devil sends pretenders. He sends them right our way; that's why we have to pay attention to our choices. It's Valentine's Day, and one year, he came out of the store with a red heart pillow, a real cute happy face, a happy smile, and happy eyes. He also brought one white rose and one red rose and a heart cookie, chocolate chip; I thought how nice this was. Then a lady, parked across from my car, saw how surprised I was, and she got out of her car and smiled and said to me, "Happy Valentine's Day." Then I screamed 'cause I'm very surprised.

I was thought about; it feels good to be thought about in a nice way. We can get smart when we are happy. When we are not too happy, that makes our thinking sometimes go to the left; then the choices we make start getting difficult. When it's time to make that good choice, you won't know it because you have been so fooled by that bad choice you made, and the other bad choice, and that other bad choice. THEN you're ready for the next choice to be a bad choice, AND it's THE GOOD ONE and YOU can't SEE IT! Those bad choices gets us in a mess and have us blind. GETTIN' STRONG, OH WELL, it's almost Valentine's Day, again, and I'm just sitting here writing to you, and he walks in my bedroom with a red rose and a card with lots of hearts on it.

Oh, how nice, I thought, to be thought about, you know what I mean, ladies, don't you? Ladies, when we are remembered in a sweet and nice way,

WE GET STRONG, WE THINK BETTER, WE ACT BETTER, WE FEEL GOOD INSIDE OUR HEARTS, AND THESE FEELINGS KEEP US HEALTHY AND ALIVE! I was once thinking about that song "REASONS." The way I get it, a part of the song says, "AFTER THE LOVE GAME HAS BEEN PLAYED, ALL OUR ILLUSIONS WERE JUST A CHARADE, AND ALL THE REASONS START TO FADE." So this is telling me that having sex with this guy, HE says, was a love game (at least he put love in there!), but, ladies, he still called sex "OUR TREASURES, OUR PERFECT STACK OF PANCAKES, A GAME! Then he goes on to say that all the reasons he was with us, all of the reasons he told us he wanted to be with us, LADIES, WAS JUST A CHARADE. (IN CASE YOU DIDN'T KNOW, CHARADE MEANS PRETENDING—HE DID NOT MEAN ANYTHING HE SAID TO US! HE ONLY WANTED THE PANCAKES WITHOUT ANY SYRUP AND ONLY LONG ENOUGH TO PLAY HIS GAME; HE CALLED IT A LOVE GAME IN THE FIRST PLACE.)

But the love game was not a love game to us; WELL, SOME OF US CALL IT A BOOTY CALL, not a game, the younger generation that is! But listen, ladies, the charade sometimes turns out to be a charade with a "HEARTBEAT," a charade with a LIFE, a HUMAN BEING (if you will). This charade is a helpless BABY with a NAME. WE DIDN'T READ BETWEEN THE LINES OR ELSE SOME OF US WOULD NOT HAVE BEEN SO BLIND ABOUT OUR TREASURES AND WHO WE GAVE THE KEY TO. HE ALSO SAYS THE "REASONS" START TO FADE. WELL, THIS BABY WILL NOT FADE; THIS BABY WILL GROW.

SO who will be there to take care of the love game as he or she grows up? NOW, what will happen to the charade baby? Will it end up in the trash dumpster or flushed somewhere or on a hospital step; WHO WILL CARE ABOUT THE CHARADE AFTER THE LOVE GAME HAS BEEN PLAYED? WHO? Are we looking at this picture like it really is? LADIES, HE WENT AFTER WE GAVE OUR PANCAKES AWAY. THERE WAS NO OTHER REASON TO BE THERE WITH US! Not even a baby. DON'T WE GET IT YET? SO, LADIES, WE CAN'T KEEP going through this life unhappy about ourselves. And when we give away the key to our treasures so easily, we become unhappy about ourselves. BELIEVE THAT! AGAIN, I say GOD is our love on any holiday. HE sends his love through different messengers, and his high favors he grants us daily. SURELY GOODNESS and MERCY shall follow us; SURELY GOODNESS and MERCY shall follow us. Just think, ladies, every step we take, GOD sends GOODNESS and MERCY right behind us! (Is that love or what?) We feel protected, don't you? You know, it's wonderful to have our good days and know it. A lot of times, we have good days, and we don't realize it! But if we're having a bad day, we surely know that without a second thought. I need to talk to you, ladies, about FAMILY. Could that be some of our downs? WELL, FAMILY is supposed to be an UP spirit in our lives. A good family to BE around should not be that hard to find. That's why our womanhood is so important.

As a little young girl in a home that seemed dysfunctional, I remember some of my first childhood days. I remember living in the projects on what they called the West Side. At that time, my oldest sister used to take me to her class in the afternoon. There was no one to watch me, and as I go further in my mind, getting older, I remember moving on the east side of town. I know more fun things happen; I went to school. The first grade class was so wonderful to me. It was like I knew I was on this earth ALIVE for the first time, so to me, things were looking up. My mother still worked, but I was in school. We had a "step" as the world calls it, "STEP FATHER." At first, I was loved by him; then the babies kept coming, so you know I ended up on the back of the bus (if you will).

But we loved my little sisters and brothers, and I still do; we have grown up in our own way. At a young age, the children lost their mother; they don't remember her at all. I tell them things about our beautiful mother; my older sisters do the same thing when they get a chance. The real hurt about my mother dying was the night she got sick on the toilet. Well, it was a Sunday night; I will never, never forget that night. She was talking about leaving THE STEPFATHER, FOR GOOD! And we were making plans to move to California where her father lived; he was still alive at that time. Well, my poor mother never made it to California; she was on the toilet talking to me and my second sister, and all of a sudden, I heard this snoring noise, and I said, "MAMA! MAMA, what are you doing?" See, she sometimes would play around with her children, from the youngest to the oldest, and there were seven of us in a three-room terrace. As hard as she worked, WHAT WAS WRONG WITH THAT PICTURE? BAD CHOICES! That's what I see!

What do you see here, ladies? Moving on, I opened the bathroom door wider, and LO AND BEHOLD, her head was lying over toward the back of the toilet; her beautiful eyes were flipping up in her head. And I screamed, "MAMA! OH, MAMA!" My second sister came in the bathroom and started throwing water in her face (YOU KNOW, LIKE YOU SEE ON TELEVISION). Finally the stepfather came to the back, where we were, and got a washcloth and kept wetting it with cold water and wiping her face. Finally she came to. She was just nervous and talking out of her head, she kept telling me "TO BE GOOD!" SEEMS I HAVEN'T BEEN GOOD YET! (SMILE.) Anyway, those were the last words my beautiful MOTHER said to me! I was told to put my mother's shoes on while we were waiting for the ambulance to come, and I could not get those shoes on her feet to save my life; those were her white work shoes, and they were too thick, so I just gave up on putting on her shoes and got up off the floor and started hugging her as she kept telling me to be good, over and over. I just could not get her to calm down; then the ambulance came, and I was told to move so they could get to my mother, and that was the last time I saw her alive.

I remember at her funeral I had on a purple dress, and a woman kept moving me around in the church. I still don't know why. Maybe because I was crying too loud. I know I wanted her to leave me alone. Anyway, I pray I see her again in heaven. (I WOULDN'T HAVE IT ANY OTHER WAY!) She is there, and I know it, so I have to make it in. BUT getting back in with the older days I need to tell you, my two older sisters became teenagers, so they didn't have to be around much; you know how teens can stay away from home. My mother never ever had a babysitter, but she kept having babies. So later on, my oldest sister was kept out of school for one year to keep an eye on my mother's babies. One day, my sister started complaining; she said, "MAMA! All the kids at school think I'm having a baby." She was able to go out even at night to the teenage dances, so everyone could see she was not having a baby. But, by my mother, taking her out of school like that, well, people talked. She had three good girlfriends. They formed a singing group called the "DELTONES." Boy, I loved them to sing; they were so good. They still sing to this day, if you asked them to or catch them in a good mood. They sung a lot of '50s songs, a lot of good songs like Frankie Lymon or The Chantels' song called "MAYBE." They were in several singing contests around our town in Denver. We always had the battle of quartet, and everyone would go to the competition every year. The DELTONES would sing. Back in those days, the town was much smaller than it is today. So everyone knew each other pretty much. I don't know why my sister's group never became famous. I think they should have left town and gone to California to become famous and then come back home. That's just my opinion. My oldest sister would always dance with the broom when *American Bandstand* was on; she was getting ready for the parties, I guess. I would just watch her and think to myself, *Is she nuts?* But I followed a lot of her footsteps growing up though because I once had a singing group when I was a teenager, called THE CHAMPELLS. I started a singing group because I loved the DELTONES so much.

We also sang in the battle of quartet; we got second place. We used to sing a lot of The Supremes songs, and we did real good with TINA TURNER's song "A FOOL IN LOVE." We didn't go any further either; most of us had to fall in love, if you want to call it that! Now I call it "fall in dumbness." But SHIRLEEN, JACKIE, NINA, AND SHARON had a happy teenage life, singing and MARCHING IN THE DRILL TEAM CALLED THE

"EAST DENVER ESCOOLITES." We were cool! And we knew it. We won lots of trophies around Colorado; all parts of Colorado did we march. We were so cute, big pretty legs in those white marching boots with green tassels in the front of our boots. And we all had to put taps on the heels of the boots so people could here our steps while watching us march.

We were so proud to be in that green-and-white uniform. With green panties underneath and a green tam on the side of our hair, we always had to be very neat and clean. If you didn't pass inspection, meaning white boots have to be shined, hair kept neat and smelling good, you would not be able to march. And as I remember, we had to have good posture at all times. It was like in the military, but we learned so much at how to be disciplined as young women.

We gave parties to raise money for uniforms, probably 10¢ to get in. And if you left the party, you had to pay a nickel to get back in. We sold chicken dinners; we even delivered them. But we all worked hard and worked together, and every girl in that drill team had her uniform. And that's all I have to say about that! I remember in my ninth grade, I did a performance with the ninth graders, and I loved it. We did the "Unsinkable Molly Brown." I got my first pair of high heels. For that performance, we performed Friday and Saturday nights, and I loved it. You couldn't have told me I was not a star because I was in on those two nights. I remember my heels were patent leather on one side and leather on the other side. Most of my life, I have always wanted to be or had to be somewhere around the stage, presenting something with somebody. It's always been in me; I don't know where I got it from really. I just love the stage. I loved to write plays and present them to a live audience. So if I found myself and my purpose here on earth then, ladies, I want to do it bigger and "MO' BETTER," so I'm going for it! Anyway, getting back to my sisters as teenagers, their poor teenage lives was just so sad to me because the next year, my mother, she took my second sister out of school; bless their hearts, I love them so much. They went through a lot as teens. Teenagers today could not go through what my sisters went through in any way, not sober.

GETTING back to my second sister, she had to stay home from school to babysit, and it was not a good thing to have them stay out of school for babies that were not theirs. And my question is why the school system didn't, back then, miss those two STUDENTS? (WHY?) The whole year, they were out of school. Why didn't someone notice? And, ladies, can't you just feel how women are always counted on to help make things better. Even as a teenager, my sisters had to be at home all day, making things better. It might have made things better for my mother, but what about the things and classes my sisters missed. Make each day count, you can't get it back. YOU FEELIN' ME!

SO you move on and try to forget the hard times, but I'm not moving on yet! The stepfather liked to drink liquor, lots of liquor. Every Friday night, his payday, we (my older sisters, Mother, and myself) were always scared to either look, speak, or go to sleep because this guy was not going to sleep. If he was drunk, some nights, he would come home and start fights with my mother for nothing. So this part of my book is called—

ALL FOR NOTHING

What I'm saying is that no one ever bothered him. He started fights for nothing. They only took him once, that I could remember, ladies. Why did my mother not leave him on the first hit? I remember, he broke a broomstick over his knee and hit my mother on the head with it; then I was running in the backdoor looking for my oldest sister, who went to call the pod, and here he came toward me, looking like a devil from hell with red eyes and gritting his teeth (like an animal). When I saw him coming toward me looking like that, MY EYES were as BIG AS TWO OREO COOKIES, AND MY HEART WAS BEATING LIKE TWELVE DRUMS OUT OF AFRICA!

And I had to go past him to get to the bed. He flipped me over a kitchen chair, and I landed on the floor and got up crying, more afraid than hurt. I got into bed so fast lightning couldn't have caught me. I pulled the cover over me, up to my eyes, making sure he wasn't coming toward me anymore. Finally, the POPO came, and he ran to the bathroom, pulled down his pants, pretending to be using the toilet; he was just sitting there scared like a snake in the grass, waiting to see who he would attack next. But, honey, let me tell you, the POPO only went in that bathroom and made his butt get up. And he said, "Can't a man use the bathroom in his own home?" This one police said, "You want to fight women, huh? FIGHT ME! FIGHT A MAN!" And the stepfather just stood there and shook with big eyes. They took him straight to jail. (DO NOT PASS GO AND COLLECT $200. [SMILE] BUT JAIL!) His children (he made with my mother) stood by the window, looking at him. My older sister said, "You, kids, come from the window." But my mother said, "NO! Let them see their father go to jail, maybe it will make him shame."

Bring Him to Shame

He was never ashamed of anything he did! AND that was a soul that hurt plenty of people on this earth before he left it. He always used to tell my mother that her three older girls were nothing but liars. My mother would say, "You better watch what you say. Those three girls you call liars might have to bring you a glass of water one day!" And sure enough at his death bed, we were giving him ice chips.

Bless Him

While he was leaving this earth, he sat up on the bed and said out loud, "HAVE MERCY ON ME!" So I think he made his peace with GOD, I pray he did. I thank our living GOD for a forgiving heart. We have to forgive each other, or he won't forgive us. NO ONE IS PERFECT! Ladies, WE MUST FORGIVE! That is so important! Keep that in your mind and heart. We feel better when we forgive, and it's so hard and heavy to carry hate and dislike around. Ladies, don't carry that, please get rid of it. That is nothing but mess, and that's all I have to say about that!

SHAME

My mind often wonders: what brings us to shame? And when we do wrong and have no shame at all, what is the "inside man" doing? I was married twice in this lifetime, and both times, no shame in anybody's game. After watching my mother's marriage with my dad (well, I was only two when they broke up for good), I was told about the fights. Ladies, she picked two fighters for husbands, AND SO DID I! Well, they picked me, but I agreed so that means I picked two fighters. Sad but it's true. AND three other females in my family did the same thing; is this a curse or what? OH GOD, let it be broken right now. Ladies, if you see yourself in any picture here, GET OUT! Call someone you know you can talk to. Some of us, well, most of us, don't have anyone we can call on and talk to about something so ugly, so humiliating, but we should. We need to be in the three place for each other.

Ladies, stop downing your sister when you know good and well she needs you. I need you to listen or just be there for a hug because you'll never know when your turn is at hand. Open up your door of "LOVE AND CARING." You are needed on the floor! GET UP, FRONT AND CENTER! Your sister needs you! So be there; GOD is there for you. AND YOU KNOW IT! I bet if my mother would have had someone to go to or listen to her "TERROR" MOMENTS she had in this world, she might have lived longer. SHE DIED AT FORTY-ONE. So young, what a short life; that's sad, isn't it, ladies? LIVE YOUR LIFE, ladies. YOU CAN'T GET IT BACK! I was only eleven when my mother died. I wish I could have been there for her, but I'm here for you! This brings me back to our choices, and that bad nasty couch is still full and crowded with people that are making BAD CHOICES. It's up to us to empty the couch; we can, you know, just by making better and wiser choices. GET ON THE GOOD COUCH NOW! IT'S TIME! GET UP! I always thought I was tough and could handle all the bad choices I made even as a little girl. Oh yes, that was my name, "TOUGH."

I always had fights with boys. I did win most of the time, except once. In high school, I had a fight with some thuglike thing that wanted to fight me because I would not be his girl. Just to look at him turned my stomach over. He blacked my eye, but he never knocked me down, believe that. If he had, you know I would have GOTTEN UP: hint! hint! Now, ladies, that was a bad choice. I did not want to, and I did not have to make and didn't make it up, and it cost me a black eye. I said to myself and GOD, as hard as I fought that monster that day, I have to fight just as hard today with wise choices. I'm really learning at my age now that I still can use my wake-up call "ring, ring, ring!" After I woke up from that last wake-up call, my three little children were all grown up.

They are on their own now with their own families; how time flies, you can't get it back. I'M LIKE, I want to teach them some more things about life. I taught them to love GOD but fear him 'cause he surely loves us. Then they were taught to work. AS LONG AS YOU WORK, YOU CAN HAVE ANYTHING YOU WANT (MY WORDS). Then I always brought them up to "watch your back." Not everyone is your friend. FRIENDS HAVE MANY DIFFERENT FACES. YOU DON'T FIGHT EACH OTHER, FIGHT FOR EACH OTHER. LOVE ONE ANOTHER; MOST OF ALL, LOVE YOU! I think I should have talked to them about love, romantic love, being in love, and how wonderful it is supposed to be and feel in your HEART when real love comes (how to be ready to enjoy love and give the love back).

The meaning of love is so misunderstood in this day and time. When will we teach our children, and I mean children, that LOVE IS NOT SEX! EVERYBODY HAS IT MIXED UP WITH I'M HIP AND COOL! LOVE IS WONDERFUL, LOVE IS HAPPINESS, LOVE IS JOY, LOVE IS TOGETHERNESS, LOVE IS QUIET, LOVE IS SOFT, LOVE IS GOD, and GOD IS LOVE. How and why do we get all those feelings mixed up? I've been talking to my boys that are men now about different kinds of KISSIN' they need to look for in a woman. I think I should have talked to my boys about sex. I did a little, and we all used to kinda giggle about who had a girlfriend or my daughter having boys calling her on the phone, but it was never serious like I know now it should have been. I should have gone into details. I was just crazy thinking their dad would talk to at least the boys about the BIRDS AND THE BEES. I felt their dad really was going to make the talk! Now I know, as an older woman, I could have done a better job teaching and telling them about sex because Dad, well, he just didn't cut the cake getting the boys ready for love, romance, and marriage. My boys could have been taken deeper into the world of females (and the different types of females) so they would be ready when the good and the bad came along.

They are "homebody" guys, far from street-ready guys, and I'm so glad about that. They are polite men and were taught to treat a female as such. And believe me, they do. MY BOYS, yes, mine, they never brought any shame to me or their father who keeps up with them to this day. I always say, "Watch how you treat your woman. YOU HAVE SISTERS AND A MOTHER, so you don't want what you put out bad to come back to you through your loved ones." I just thank my GOD they are hardworking GENTLEMEN. NO SHAME!

My Womb! My Womb!

One of the most wonderful days I had here on earth was the time I went to Vegas for my oldest son's wedding. We were in my hotel room—the RIVIERA HOTEL, if you will. My sons went to the other hotel to bring their clothes over where I was so we all could spend the night in my room. I was on the fourth floor, and the windows had long beautiful wall-to-wall drapes, and the big-picture window, you could just slide it open and look out at all of Vegas. I had never been to Las Vegas, so I was on cloud nine thousand. I looked out the window to see if I could see my sons, and I did.

A bus had just let a bunch of people off in front of my window straight down, but I could see my sons. I put my head out of the window, saw my two handsome sons with white sleeveless T-shirts on big muscles, big shoulders out, handsome haircuts, AND MY HEART REJOICED. Then the next thing I knew, I just felt wonderful and happy, and I YELLED OUT AS LOUD AS I COULD, "MY WOMB, MY WOMB. THEY CAME FROM MY WOMB!" Everyone looked up! No doubt wondering who was yelling such a thing in Vegas, my sons looked up too. "MOM," they said and just started shaking their heads, laughing. That was one of the most wonderful moments of my life thus far. And I'll never forget the timing and the feelings I had at that precious moment; no one could ever buy it from me in two lifetimes. And that's all I have to say about that!

My Girl

Never think I was going to forget to tell you about my oldest child; my daughter, she has a beautiful name, KATRINA! She is so good; she was born at the most perfect time in my life. Everybody was happy, seems the world was good and peaceful and quiet. So lovely, so lovely, I was in my hospital room holding her, looking at how beautiful she is. Her nose, her little hands and feet; it was a beautiful time to be a woman. I went to the window; it was snowing ever so peacefully. I had a little transistor radio (that's what they called it in those days anyway).

And the radio played a song with the cutest music to it called "MELLOW YELLOW." I didn't know what it meant, but the music was so nice, and I looked at her, and she was just sleeping in my arms so safe and warm. Ladies, can we feel safe and warm today? HOW MUCH DOES IT COST? I'll buy it, will you? The question is, where do we buy it? Well, on her thirtieth birthday, I found that song "Mellow Yellow" on a CD, and I pray and hope when she ever feels she's not safe and warm, she will pull that CD out and play it and know that her mother is with her through GOD and that she is SAFE AND WARM! She grew up so cute with fat yellow legs, and today, she looks a lot like my mother; she has my mother's long thick hair, and her hands are just like Mama's. KATRINA is a smart lady, and she is a hard worker; I had her join in all kinds of talent things, YOU KNOW HOW MOTHERS DO! She was in the NATIONAL TEENAGE MISS AMERICA PAGEANT, DRILL TEAMS, CHEERLEADER, and SHEENWAY DANCERS IN HOLLYWOOD.

NOW SHE works at a bank, and she's a mother and a wife, a real good wife, a better wife than her mother was! I never did follow the orders, but I did try. Some are ready, some are not! But my baby was ready to be a homemaker, and she is happy doing everything she is into. So that means I'm well with her happiness.

Green Is Good

I want to write to you, ladies, on the subject GREEN IS GOOD! When we see green, why do we know and recognize GREEN IS GOOD? Well, green is the color of what? MONEY! So that leads us to green as a good word, like glad green money (smile). GREEN is such a pleasant color. The GREEN forest is beautiful, isn't it? The GREEN grass we can sit, lie, or stand on. It's not a bad place to be, ON THAT GREEN GRASS! BUT! THOUGHT! Don't let the green grass fool ya! THE GRASS IS GREENER ON THE OTHER SIDE! NO, you ought to see the water bill. If the other side had been watered and cared for, it would be just as GREEN as all the other grass, NOW WOULDN'T IT? GOD made GREEN grass good. No matter what color we have in our living rooms, the GREEN plants make it look so elegant and beautiful. The GREEN LIGHT at the corner means go! We love to go! Everyone loves to go! When we see that GREEN LIGHT, we know go, which makes us happy. So when we know GREEN is good, ladies, look always for the good, and usually, you'll find GREEN around. You know how we just love plants, REAL or SILK. They make us happy as we look at the beauty of them. GREEN BEAUTIFIES.

NOW, ladies, when we are showered with LOVE, KIND WORDS, PEACE, SELF-CONFIDENCE, PRIDE, and LAUGHTER, we look good in every room, just like the color GREEN! GREEN STANDS OUT!

GREEN SHOWS UP! GREEN will speak out when it is taken good care of. THE color GREEN is GOOD; GREEN HOLDS YOUR GROUND! Ring, ring. Wake-up call!

Out of Order

Ladies, let's go there for a bit. There are so many times that our GOD came to us in some kind of way and gave us SIGNS, HINTS, KNOCKS, and BUMPS AGAIN, AGAIN and AGAIN TO LET US KNOW that we are OUT OF ORDER! Some of us are waaaaaay OUT OF ORDER and don't care. WE won't listen and have completely stopped trying. WE get all these warning signs from GOD himself, but we keep sitting on that "BAD COUCH." YES, even with all the warnings, we sit on that "BAD COUCH" anyway!

Ladies, if we let bad things stop us, we won't be here for the good things. We know we don't like being on that "BAD COUCH," but we are so "OUT OF ORDER," we don't realize where we are sitting. RING, RING. Wake-up call! When you don't care how you look or smell, YOU'RE OUT OF ORDER! When we don't have a place to live, OUT OF ORDER! When we don't have a vision for our future or our children's future, OUT OF ORDER! When we have no education, OUT OF ORDER! No job, no income, OUT OF ORDER! NO family or friends, OUT OF ORDER! NO church or home, OUT OF ORDER! NO BISHOP or PASTOR you can call on when you need to, OUT OF ORDER! (You need that!) IF YOU ARE MARRIED and YOUR HUSBAND does NOT WORK and IS UNWILLING AND UNABLE to take care of you MENTALLY or PHYSICALLY—FINANCIALLY NOT READY, YOU'RE OUT OF ORDER! IF you don't insist that he get a job and do better for you both, YOU'RE OUT OF ORDER! (REMEMBER we can do bad by ourselves.) But we (well, most of us) don't like being by ourselves. SO, ladies, if you have a man, help HIM to help YOU SO HE can HELP YOU! Ladies, you can't do it all! AND IF YOU WANT TO DO IT ALL, YOU'RE OUT OF ORDER! I NEED TO GO TO THE BIG LETTERS FOR THIS NEXT MESSAGE!

Run

Ladies, you're not his mother; you're his wife. Stop blocking him from being all he can be. NOW LISTEN UP! Ladies, stop giving up your paycheck while he sits home, doing sweet nothing. Insist that he has a payday too. Ladies, stop buying clothes, cars, and stop buying those sheets, ladies, when you know very well you're not the only one sleeping on them. Ladies, if he can't love GOD, he really can't love you either! (Sad but it's true.) If he does not love himself, then you're in the BACK of the bus. I know from my own walking-in-darkness experience!

Ladies, if he does not take care of himself, he won't and can't take care of you. (Simple as that!) When we meet our men for the first time, we say "Oh, he's so cute. Girl, he's fine. He's got pretty white teeth too. He is so built and got that six-pack. Oh, his chest and arms, he is it. He's fly, that's him for me!" OH, and if we find out he's in church, THAT'S IT! IS that all we need to know, ladies? NO! NO ! NO! NO! WE need to know about his love, his heart for GOD, his love for his mother, and how he treats or has treated his mother because, you can believe me, you will be loved the same way he loves and treats his mother. If he has a mother (pray he does), you can watch him as you mark your weights and measures. GOD wants us to use our weights and measures! I kid you not. This is being a wise woman, a "finally paying attention" woman, a "thinking with our head instead of our pancakes" WOMAN! (Are you with me on this part, sisters?)

SISTER, SISTER, SISTER! IF you meet a man and he does not own a TV, A CAR, OR A WRISTWATCH, RUN! Because if you don't, you will usually end up buying him shoes, socks, and underwear. Nothing wrong, ladies, buying him shoes, socks, and underwear 'cause, GUESS WHAT, we have to let him know off the top: WE LIKE STOCKINGS, HEELS, AND PRETTY DRESSES TOO! AND SLIP a NICE Cuddly COAT in the conversation (GOT MINK!)

We Got It

We are usually left holding the bag, buying everything with our money. RING, RING. Some of our men don't think, and they that did not have parents, teach them that one day, they will fall in love and maybe be the head of their own house. Those are the men we have to raise as though we birth them. Speaking of BIRTHING THEM, we go ahead and bring their children into the world, and WE ALL go to our DEATHBEDS bringing a life into the world. Mother's Day comes, and he forgets to buy a card, etc. Now why is that, ladies? We put up with what they bring to us; we can't accept that from our men. They seem to get away with so much—"I FORGOT" or "I CAN'T" and "DON'T BOTHER ME!" or "YOU TRIPPIN', GIRL!"

And we take them by the hand and say, "That's okay, babe. I GOT IT!" Even the real ugly men get away with such ways. "YEAH, WE GOT IT ALL RIGHT!" We gotta get busy and wake up and demand to be provided for and loved MO' BETTER! We gotta know that we walked beside our men; we don't want to be in front. GOD did not mean for us to be in front of our men. And he did not mean for us to step up front and pay the rent ALONE or step up front and buy the family car ALONE or buy the food in the house ALONE. We pay utility bills ALONE, fix up the living quarters ALONE, drive to work in bad weather ALONE, get our car fixed ALONE, change a flat tire ALONE. Most of us can change a flat tire; there are a lot of ladies who really know how to change a flat tire now. We don't like to change flat tires, but it was a job we were pushed into because there was not a man responsible enough to change a flat tire. So again, we have to do what we have to do by any means necessary, got that, ladies! And some of us have our babies ALONE, always go to the doctor ALONE, and the majority of us ladies surely go to church ALONE. And while he's resting in, we are doing most of these things. At least four days a week. We don't want to be mean and hateful sisters (that's not the point here), it's just that we need to know we are being treated FAIRLY, loved FULLY, and appreciated truly. THAT'S THE POINT! You and I know we will always do our fair share and some. We keep things going right in our homes; that is our motto! So, ladies, we must, in this day and time, get and demand our men to do better and to step it up! We all witnessed our new president get elected, and he is only one man, so if one man can do what he set out to do, that tells us all men can do what they set out to do in this world. What one man can do, another can do! And that's real. So men, the ladies are serving notice to you today. We need you to truly STEP IT UP!

Step It Up

I often wonder why I was not asked to step it up when I was younger. Why didn't anyone ask me, when I get older, what would I like to be to make my money in this life? No one asked. Being only eleven years old when my mother died, I just did not get a good start. My real father remarried and had other children, so he wasn't paying any attention to me or my two older sisters. So we kinda felt our way through this world. As three young girls lost, broke, but determined to stay together, my older sister got a job after she graduated from high school; she started working at the Hilton Hotel's laundry department. It was time to step it up! But everywhere we went, they would not rent us a place to live because we were too young. So later on when my sister became eighteen years old, finally!

And she got married, and then we were able to get our own apartment. WE LOVED IT! Once we got used to our apartment, life was normal and happy. My brother-in-law was wonderful to us; it was like we knew him all our lives. Then after a year in the apartment, we moved into the house of my brother-in-law's parents. He grew up in that house, so it was kind of old, but we were glad to clean it up and move in; it only had two bedrooms, so my middle sister and I shared our room, and we loved it. A few years had passed on, and both sisters were having a baby. Now we wished our mother really could have been alive to see this, both her older daughters having a baby!

It was so funny at first to see both the big bellies. Then one day, I came home from my drill team practice, and as soon as I opened the front door, you could see all the way straight through the house. I could see the kitchen, and lo and behold, they were standing in front of the stove, and my second sister's blouse was on fire. Then my oldest sister yells out, "TEAR YOUR BLOUSE OFF, TEAR YOUR BLOUSE OFF!" So they both took their blouses off, and water was everywhere. They were throwing water trying to put the flame out, so both of them were wet, and I mean wet from the hair down. And then they tore their blouses off, and I looked at them; they were both standing there with these two big BELLIES hanging out. I could not keep from laughing. I SAID, "WHAT IN THE WORLD ARE YOU TWO DOING?" They were kind of laughing and crying at the same time. They were painting, and the paint thinner was on the stove and then POOF! But thank you, GOD, they did not get hurt! I TOLD YOU GOD HAD US ALL THE TIME AND WE DIDN'T KNOW IT! But really and truly, our little house on Lafayette Street was the most joyful place to be back then. You always heard laughter, jokes, music, and singing. We even had a piano that was left in the house, and plenty of people used to come over and play it. I remember Philip Bailey and Maurice White, BETTER KNOWN AS EARTH, WIND & FIRE, coming over, singing with my first brother-in-law named MORRIS CUMMINGS. Now he has a singing group called the MARVELL'S; they made a record called the "MIRACLE OF LIFE." I still have the forty-five records, and it still sounds beautiful as it did the first time I heard it. I can surely say he missed his call from the singing world. Anyway, lots of singing would really be happening then. We always had Christmas parties, baby showers, and dinners. Oh, and don't leave out the "BID WIZ" card playing that went on almost every weekend. There were card-playing clubs, weight watchers clubs. Everybody just loved our home; we finally had a happy home.

We can say our life was finally steppin' up! I used to love it when my brother-in-law would wake up on Saturday mornings and have the breakfast food smelling so good you could smell it down the block. Then in the afternoon, you would hear THE FAMOUS BOBBY BLUE BLAND playing as you walked toward the front door. Oh, I loved my life at that moment and time, BUT YOU CAN'T GET IT BACK! SO MAKE EACH DAY COUNT! But I will always have the happiness of those moments in my heart always. I remember when my sister put new furniture in layaway, and we got to have a new couch and chair set, a new TV, and new beds 'cause those beds my mother had us sleeping in, well, we won't go there, okay! Ladies, just because it's where we come from does not mean we have to stay there. And this world is a big, big place, and we are to go out and conquer every good thing that GOD has put here for us to be happy, joyful, and pretty. ALL UP IN IT!

No matter what we look like, we can fix it up with makeup, eyeliner, lipstick, and blush. There is makeup for everyone in every color. Whether you're skinny or fat, there are nice, pretty, cute, and glamorous clothes for everyone. You have to look and find your size and color. Every girl can't look her best in every color; we all have a special color that brings out our womanhood, our beauty, and our strength while other colors can bring out our weakness. So make sure you know your colors so that you can be ladies as all of you should be, got to be, and better be. WE LOVE OURSELVES, REMEMBER!

Ladies, we have to know our touch-tones, so we need to pay attention to who we are around. We can't use bad language, please watch that tongue! That's why GOD put teeth in our mouth, not just to chew food but to put a gate around our danger tongue so we can lock it up when it wants to say things it does not need to say. Our teeth are there to keep that tongue quiet. GOD says LOCK IT DOWN! That's why the tongue is in the middle, and our top and bottom teeth shut together to make the tongue be still. IT'S CALLED SHUT THE GATE!

Do you have the vision, ladies? Even when we hear bad pronunciation of words, you don't want to be around that every day. Birds of a feather will flock together! If you don't know how to pick such touch-tones, start praying more and ask for guidance and order of your steps. GOD will show you if you ask; SO ASK! This way, you won't worry about what you teach your children. I asked GOD to put me in a better path, and he did. I just wish I would have asked him in the early part of my life. So maybe YOU have time to make it count! SO ASK! Ladies, it's so good and fun to speak better, to learn and know when we're in and around some good FOUNDATION; REMEMBER THAT WORD? If you're in their place, it will rub off on you too, so stay around and find your path. You will know it, and when you do, put YOUR BEST FOOT FORWARD, and you're in there!

Stuck Like Glue

We stuck together like glue and made life happier than we had ever been. My other sister got married later down the line, and me, I got a job at FURR's cafeteria at fifteen years old. So we turned out better than people thought we would. With no mother or father around, we were in God's holy hands, and he brought us through the tunnel. My question is why or where was our village? We had no one to ask about college; we didn't know how to apply, which meant we were not going. My sisters would have and could have gone only if a grown-up person would have given a little direction on education or anything to be a better person in society.

I watched judges on TV, and they always asked the teenagers that come in their courtroom, "What do you want to be when you get older?" Some don't know, but usually, they do ask them. A lot of people knew we had just lost our mother. "Why wasn't there a village waiting to help direct our path?" That is all any child needs—a caring village. One of our aunts told us to get an old man to marry us. Now doesn't that sound like a scene in *The Color Purple*? What I'm talking about is real here. Ladies, she said we would be taken care of by an older man. I could not stand for an old man to touch me. I get ready to throw up just at the thought of one bothering me in that way! To me that is sick, and the worse advice you could give anyone. And that was our blood aunt saying that to us, isn't that sad? I just became a GREAT, GREAT aunt; my niece Nicole gave us little Zoey. I know GOD shined on me and my sisters; we lived to have the title GREAT, GREAT AUNT. GOD said he will show you GENERATIONS, and again, we have to love him right 'cause he loves us more than right. I can't even hear myself telling my nieces or any young person that looks to me for wisdom or any advice about their future. If that is the best advice I could give them, with no wisdom at all, I would just keep my tongue behind the gate of my teeth and keep it shut!

That is not leading and guiding the next generations toward positive goals for their future. Directions like that will surely head one to destruction, just NO WISDOM passed on at all! But my sisters and I turned out okay anyway. My daughter says, "Mom, you want to control me and my life." I guess I wanted to protect her as a mother since I did not have a mother's love and guidance; I was protecting her in the wrong way as far as she sees it. To me if I had control, I would have her somewhere in New York dancing with the ROCKETTS. If I were in control, she would own her own PENTHOUSE APARTMENT. If I were in control of her life, she surely would not have to work two jobs to make ends meet.

I would have a better plan instead of work, work, work then die; that's the wrong way, and I'm pointing the arrow the other way, but she thinks she is on the right road and my thoughts are nuts. I know I was not a perfect mother; half the time I didn't really know what I was doing. I just, most of the time, followed what my older sisters did, which was what I thought good, strict but good with the kids. Maybe I was not going about motherhood in a good way, but I thought I was. I put her in the Miss Teenage America pageant, cheerleading in school, and private dance lessons she really did not want to take.

But she had such beautiful legs. I just knew she could make good money dancing professionally with good training. I wanted her to have a life of good standing and know she could do something else besides having babies and go to the day care every day. I was trying to let her see and be exposed to a different kind of life. All of us got married and had babies. But there are other things to do in this life when you are young and you have someone to point you in the positive direction. Then you later have your families and settle down after you have found someone, and did YOU! Because when the babies start coming, the traveling is pretty much over unless you have planned together and saved together. I did not get to do some of the things I'm writing about, so I just thought my daughter could enjoy a little bit of the limelight. I love my grandchildren very much, and I love my son-in-law; he's learned more from watching what she did.

She was a good mother. My mother was loving and beautiful, very, very beautiful! She just picked the wrong man, that's why, ladies. We have to watch them before we marry them because you can be good in your heart, just like my mother was; she didn't drink liquor; she didn't smoke cigarettes nor did drugs. She liked to sing, dress up, and wear her hats. She always wanted her three older girls to sing in a group together like the "LENNON SISTERS." They could harmonize together real pretty. And we would watch them on TV every Saturday night. That was one of the luxuries we had in the hell house: we could watch TV on Saturday night because on Friday night, Stepfather was out in the bar drinking. And we love for him to be out drinking just so he wouldn't be home, but he always had to come back home.

That was the problem. And now I'm in this other tunnel. I love to eat sweets; it's hard not to, but we have to do it. I've been getting in the swimming pool. I'm forty pounds in the water, with no pain in the knees. Yes! I'm learning to shop and buy healthy foods. *Don't bring any sweets home*, I tell myself. This week, I was strong, left the sweets at the store. I'm really trying to keep busy these days with other things—my plays and my book—so my mind will not want to eat anything sweet. See, I don't want the sweets; my mind wants them. It's a mind war. Maybe I need to be hypnotized. HA AAAAAAAH! That's a thought! I got to keep going, ladies, no matter what, if you are here. Don't give up! We can come out of this tunnel together. We will come out together; we can come out together because we're getting up, REMEMBER? And we're getting out of the tunnel. AND THAT'S REAL.

CLICK

I was watching a movie the other day called *Click*; it's a remote to your life, good and bad. You can click forward, or you can click backward. I've thought what I'd be like if I had a remote control like that in real life. I know what I would change in my life; what would you change? See, with this remote, you could go anywhere you wanted to go in your life. I would want to be born again. I love my mother! I love my father too! But maybe I would put myself in a different smarter womb. Then maybe I would be somewhat different and not inherit all the bad things. BUT GOD KNEW EXACTLY WHERE HE WANTED ME TO BE PLACED. I feel I got more bad parts of the DNA from my mother and father. But you can't get it back.

That was only a song, but ladies, it did make me think deep, and I like to think. I write and direct plays a lot, so I know I like to think more than the average person. I'd say I haven't reached the peak of my writing days yet; I'm nowhere near where I intend to be. I keep thinking Tyler Perry started small, so I'll just keep writing and directing. We have a good time on stage. We have a real fun drama ministry here in our city of Denver. And if God's will be done, we will one day go out with his message. I guess I've always wanted to direct something. When I was little, I always had the neighborhood kids marching in a line. Anything fun, fun is important to our happiness, ladies. Sometimes I would form clubs, kind of like *The Little Rascals* on TV. We had money in our little bank jar until my friend's brother found it in her room, took the whole jar to the candy store, and brought candy, and that was the end of the club.

So I was always thinking of something to do in our little hood. One time, we made a tetherball out of socks and played on the corner stop sign, which was our pole. Now when the Hula-Hoop came out, I was the best, believe me! I could work that Hula from my hips to my neck, from my ankles back up to my hips. Then I would put one arm in and go down again, and put one leg in and just Hula with one leg. You name it. I could work it! And now I'm old.

(Smile!) But through the grace of God, my sisters and I outlived our mother and father. So we knew we wanted to do something different from our poor wonderful mother, who died so very young. She worked all the time; maybe she was just tired of the marriage, the husband, and the children. We don't know, but she prayed all the time, I surely remember that. Every night, she would be on the side of her bed on her knees, so she is with our God; I know she is. Plus her heart was so good toward other people, and God loves a pure heart. HE said so! That's what he's coming back after his church, our clean pure hearts. LOVE YOU, DEARLY MAMA.

Traveling Light

OH, ladies, I got to tell you one more thing about Mr. Friday Night Special (THE STEPFATHER). He came in big and bad on Fridays. You know, PAYDAY, had to have his liquor in him. Well, the very last time he ran me, my two older sisters, and my mother out of the house, we had made a promise that the next time he came home drunk and crazy, we were not going to run. We were tired of having to run out in the snow, freezing and walking until my mother found somewhere for us to sleep-over my aunt's house or a friend's house; we were just fed up with all of that madness. One time, he hit my middle sister in her mouth with his fists and busted her lips so damn bad. She could not go to work for a week, and Mama did not call the popo either! Why, I will never know; how could she let him get away with such a horrible thing, hitting her child like that.

Did she love him that much, ladies? Or was she thinking with and loving her pancakes instead of a mother's love with her child? Maybe she was just afraid of him because violent men do frighten women and we can't beat them up or outbox them, but we can surely hurt them or kill them. But who wants to kill their husband? Not me! Not you, they are not worth it anyway. Our freedom means more than anything. So maybe my mother was just thinking about her freedom. We don't know; only God knows everything. And so we have to be at peace with that, okay? But he hit my sister on her mouth. I remember my sister went over her friend's house to stay. I was crying; I wanted to go with her, but she told me no. Anyway we were tired of him, the drinking and the cursing, and we said we were not going to run anymore even if we had to go to jail. Especially my oldest sister, she was so tired of him and was embarrassed in front of her friends (if they came to our house).

Most of the time, they would wait on the front porch. So my oldest sister, she had made her peace with God and said it was okay; so we were just going to kill him. We had pop bottles as weapons, ice picks, one hammer, and a hatchet and a knife. I was only about nine or ten years old, but we weren't running anymore. We had made up our minds; we were well with whatever it took for this madness to stop once and for all. My mother was ready too! THAT'S RIGHT! She's the one that got us in that hell. So it came down to kicking asses and taking names later. We went to bed that night with our clothes on; we always knew it was a risk to sleep without your clothes on Fridays. So we had clothes on.

God says, "Put on the whole armor." Well, we thought we had our armor on when Mr. Friday Night Special came home. We were ready for WAR; we were ready for JAIL, and we were ready for HORROR! And he was just as nice and sweet, did not say any curse words to my mother, but he never ever knew to this day that we had prepared for him to die. And, ladies, he never ever came home fussing and cussing at us again, so it had to be GOD! That's why God is so REAL; he didn't want us to go through life with that over our heads and in our hearts. When you serve the devil, you have a HEAVY HEART, so as for me, I'm traveling light! And, ladies, YOU CAN TOO!

My Dreams, My Thoughts

Ladies, let's think about our dreams and how to make some or all of them come true. If you don't have a man or a husband, WHO ARE YOU? I'll ask, WHO ARE WE? As one woman, what shall we do with us? If *us* means *just me*, then what shall I do with *me*? Can I make *me* happy? Of course, I can! I've been working at it real hard. The things that I want to do are (1) love myself better and (2) read God's word more. I have to find the rest of me, and I know I'm in my Bible. I love to decorate things—houses, apartments, churches, etc., and I love shopping. It cheers me up so good and wonderful. I feel rejuvenated when I shop and meet new people. Oh, and when I give a play. I'm on cloud nine thousand and one; I love entertaining anyway. I love giving my two older sisters parties or surprising them with girl stuff; we just laugh. I love MY PASTOR and his wife SISTER DALLAS so much I pray for them three times a day every day. When I see them, they are very happy. I just had a surgery; I think it took about four or five hours. And my pastor is so wonderful. He came to the hospital and sat with my family and stayed. Even though I had already gone into surgery, he stayed with my family. He is so good and precious to us; we have to pray for him nonstop just because he's so good to people most of the time. We can't take a chance and let the enemy use him or even think he can come near this great man of God.

He was truly sent and called by God. You know how I know? Because his tree is full of all kinds of good fruit. So we just thank God for him; he reminds me so much of our recently elected president, the way he brings God's word forth. He truly feeds us the word of God when you leave his presence. If you're not full, then you weren't hungry at all. And that's all I have to say about that. I really love my brothers-in-law, BOBBY and ROYAL, and they are real good to my sisters; they are pretty happy. So I'm good with that. Right now I'm married to Jesus. He's the rock of my family, the one that holds everything I do together. He takes real good care of me, like I said earlier in this book, he always has. I just didn't know it right off, but I know now!

I was saying to my sister in the lord, BARBARA JEAN, that God has been so good to us. As kids, we played together for years, and now, we can talk on the phone. Even though we don't see each other too much anymore, we care about each other. Then we have our other sister in the lord, PEARL; she is as beautiful as her name, in and out. She and I try to make sure we keep the schoolgirls in touch as much as we can. Everyone brings a dish of whatever they want to cook, and we laugh, eat, talk, and dance if we want to! But God blessed us to still be here together so we don't take it lightly, we're making it count! Dreams do come true if you believe and act on what you believe in. When we schoolgirls are together, our dream is real; we are there with each other, so the dream came true because we put our belief into action! And, ladies, that's called MAKING IT COUNT!

RED ROOSTER

My oldest sister sometimes talks about the time when we were young and living with my mother and her husband (I'LL BE NICE). Well, she used to tell some of the kids that she got a bike for Christmas, knowing she only got nothing. No, I take that back. One Christmas, she and my second sister got a sweater, and the other year, as they were teenagers, they both got a watch. So Mama did try, didn't she? I remember as being the third sister and the baby of the three of us, for Christmas one year, my mother brought me a black tight skirt with a red rooster on it, and it had a red rooster belt that came with it. I was in the sixth grade. I said, "Mama, is this really my present?" She replied, "Yes!" So I held the skirt up and turned my lips upside down; I said, "I don't want this tight skirt, Mama! And it's got a red rooster on it. This is ugly." So I cried because I didn't have any other present for Christmas. My oldest sister, she loved the skirt set. It was a skirt set, as I remember, because it had a red blouse with roosters all over it. So I let her have it; she was so happy. I didn't want it. It fit her perfectly. She looked real cute in it just like a teenager; they liked that kind of stuff. I didn't; I was a girl that always had fights with boys. I liked jeans and pants; you know, I was in sixth grade. I truly was not into tight skirts. In those days, a girl did not want to show what she was made of or her good shape she had, if she had one! Not in the sixth grade! That just wasn't happening then, but it is now!

Ladies, why is it that now in this generation that our females seem to be so hot with body heat for guys without any shame or shyness? Where is our innocence? I often say to myself, *Is it the short skirts and boots the ladies wear? Or it has to be the thong panties 'cause the younger ladies surely buy them and wear them a lot.* Now there has to be a sex spirit in those thongs because the thong is always touching the main parts of the pancake at all times, more so when we walk or dance. By the time a slow dance is over, well, we're ready for him (little does he know, his work is already done) because we got something rubbing us, giving out sexual feelings and sex thoughts through the whole dance. And a guy won't have to say or do too much after a slow dance or a fast dance. Blouses are low in and out of school, in and out of church.

Half the time, I can't tell the Christian from the worldly people. Everybody has something to show. And when you look at the pregnant young ladies, the blouses are so tight you see the big belly and the big navel that used to be something for the husband to see, not the town square. Ladies, let's put our sex back in the bedrooms. This is the way we are surely losing our respect; if we don't show we have respect for ourselves, how can anyone else show any respect for us? WE have to get it back like it was written to be—WOMEN in their place as clean women. Don't get me wrong here, ladies. Yes, sex is beautiful BUT not to be sold nor to be popular with it, not to be with a man that we know we have to share with fifteen or twenty other women; NOW this thought is so crazy. THINK ABOUT THIS, LADIES, EVERYBODY gets my germs whether they know me or not! I get their germs because I want them NO MATTER WHAT! THERE is a DEADLY SPIRIT out there; its name is AIDS. He comes to STEAL, KILL, AND DESTROY!

Ladies, this is real, and there is no THONG or GOOD FEELING on this earth worth SUFFERING FOR! I have seen them get boils all over their faces and probably all over their whole bodies. Big ugly sores full of puss and germs, plus all the other hurting mess that a lot of our women AND MEN go through BEFORE THEY DIE! All because they felt sexy! Ladies, this is not the deal; this is not how GOD planned it for us. This is how the enemy from hell had planned to get us with the THONGS, short tight skirts, and tight jeans that rub us all day at work to keep our minds on YOU KNOW WHO FOR YOU KNOW WHAT! THAT'S what we call a QUIET TEMPTATION; HAVE TO KEEP THAT LOOKOUT, LADIES! Pay ATTENTION TO THE FEELINGS YOU HAVE WHEN YOU HAVE YOUR CLOTHES ON OR OFF! The ENEMY is waiting to catch us OFF GUARD! DON'T FORGET THIS, LADIES! IT'S A MATTER OF LIFE AND DEATH! SO IF YOU SEE THAT RED ROOSTER, SEND HIM HOME! Getting back to me not having a nice Christmas, I was really sad. So anyway, I walked out the back door and down the alley. I went to my girlfriend Shirleen's house. WHICH TAKES US TO, THE CHAMP IS COMING.

The Champ Is Coming, The Champ Is Coming

Yes, that was my best friend Shirleen; she lived down the alley. I went over there almost every day of my childhood; we were teenagers together. We did sing in a girls' group together, with Jackie and Sharon. I mentioned earlier in the book. We were called The Champells; we had such fun singing around Denver. We sang at the Holiday Inn, CARPENTERS' HALL, and THE GRANGE HALL. THOSE were pretty popular places to be in DENVER in those good old days. I remember we had on hot pants.

That was the style at that time, hot pants. They were pink, with the top to match, and we had worn tall boots with that outfit. Oh, we thought we were something, and we were. We could harmonize so beautiful. We would sing at school, and all the kids, well, teenagers would gather around us in the park when we would sing at lunchtime, and we love the attention. But getting back to walking out on my mother on Christmas morning, that skirt really upset me. So I got to Shirleen's house, and in her yard, she and her sister were playing tetherball that they got for Christmas; and they even got a pole that came with it. They were just laughing and hitting the ball around the pole as I stepped in their backyard. So I watched for a bit; then the next thing I knew I was storming up that alley like I was going to beat someone up. I went in the back door. I said, "Mama!" I SHOUTED, "Shirleen and Waltereen got a tetherball and a pole for Christmas AND I'M THE CHAMP." See, no one at any school could beat me at tetherball. No one! I was taken by my gym teacher, Mr. Wilson, to schools all over the city and OUT of the city to all kinds of tetherball tournaments. I went to schools I never even heard of before to play; all kinds of girls were there. I played some tall girls, looking to be about six or seven feet tall at that time. That was tall, real tall, and they thought they could beat me easy because I was shorter than them. But I KICKED BUTT on the tetherball.

I was just unbeatable for some reason; I guess God had me then. And I didn't know it, but I do now! None of them could not beat me. I always knew in my mind the way I would beat them. See, I would not even let them get the ball back. Once I put my hands on it, I just knew how to win. And I would wrap that ball around the pole so fast. They couldn't see it to hit it. THE GAME WAS OVER (smile!). And that's why I say, THE CHAMP IS COMING, THE CHAMP IS COMING because that's who I was at that time in my life, A CHAMP! I was always pretty good at most of the sports I played, except running a fifty-yard dash. I could never beat Vickie, another close, close girlfriend I grew up with; we still talk a lot on the phone to this day. I needed the tetherball; that's what I felt in my heart. We always made a ball out of socks and played in the front outside on the stop sign. We needed those socks on our feet, and believe me, we were without so many things when it came to clothes, and pj's, we were without. Someone asked the question, "How are you doing?" The answer was, "I'M DOING WITHOUT!" because, ladies, we did do without. Anyway, after I yelled at my mother about being the champ WITHOUT a tetherball, she went in her pocket. She always wore those house dresses with pockets. She pulled out two dollars and gave me that! I remember grinning and running out of the back door down the alley, put the money in my shoe, and beat Shirleen and her sister in tetherball all Christmas day! I was happy! BEING A WINNER MAKES YOU HAPPY.

Tea Time

I really loved Shirleen's parents; she had a nice mother and a nice father. They let me eat over their house a lot, and every year, Mrs. Jones (that's Shirleen's mother) would make sure I went to the mother-and-daughter tea at school; I used to like that. My mother always had to work, so she could never, ever take me. But Mrs. Jones made sure I got there. I always wore my Easter dress! As I got older, even as a married woman, I would go over to the Joneses' house. Mr. Jones was quite old, and he would ask me the same question all the time, just to get him a good laugh. HE WOULD ASK ME IF I WAS STILL MARRIED. AND I WOULD ASK HIM, "WHAT DAY OF THE WEEK IS IT?" AND HE WOULD SAY SATURDAY, AND I ALWAYS REPLIED, "I'M NEVER MARRIED ON SATURDAYS!"

And he would hold his stomach and laugh so hard and long; I was glad I could give him a good laugh. He was a nice man and took good care of his family; they always had a happy home, that's why I was over there so much! And I loved Shirleen until the day God called her, and I still love her. But anyhow, you can see, ladies, that I needed a vision. My mother did the best she knew to do, but I knew I had to and could do mo' better. So I always used to say to my mother, "I'M NEVER GETTING MARRIED. I'M NEVER HAVING CHILDREN!" She always laughed at me. I guess I made her happy because she sure used to laugh hard when I would say that! Sometimes she would come out of the clear blue sky and ask me if I was going to get married, and when I yelled "HECK, NO," boy, would she laugh. (She always sipped on a cup of hot tea and gave us, girls, tea and toast.) I have always had to keep tea in my house; as a woman, it is so peaceful to relax with a cup of tea after you have got through your hard day at work or even a good long day of shopping. I have all kinds of tea, and I really love the strawberry tea (if you have not had any, try it); it's a happy tea, makes me very joyful. I think GOD gave us tea to show his love and closeness to us.

Heck, No!

Ladies, that's not a bad thing to say NO; *NO* can save us from so many things. *NO* has a track record of being THE GOOD, THE BAD, and THE UGLY! BUT *NO* CAN GET US RESPECT!

NO CAN GET US PEACE OF MIND!

NO CAN GET US TO OUR GOALS!

NO CAN SAVE US FROM HEARTBREAK!

NO CAN MAKE US SMART!

NO CAN MAKE US THANKFUL!

NO CAN KEEP US ALIVE!

NO CAN MAKE US RICH IN SO MANY WAYS! And last of all,

NO CAN GET US CLOSER TO GOD!

Ladies, there are so many people who don't like the word *NO*! NOT EVER!

Some of us are programmed to think *NO* is a word we really don't need.

Ladies, we need *NO* more than you will ever KNOW! We can save a lot of ugly things from coming our way with *NO*! It's not bad to say that word and stick to it.

We say it, *NO*! but don't mean it.

We all understand that the opposite of *NO* is *YES*! NOW, *YES* is a good word too!

But for some reason, when we hear or say the word *YES*, usually we regret it later down the line. Now the words have not done a thing to us. It's what follows the *YES'S* and *NO'S* that start all the mess!

THE MESS!

I had one of my nieces. Well, I have several nieces, and I love them all dearly, and I always want the best for them just like anyone would for their nieces or family members. We all give them advice as being older and wiser; we are out of place if we don't tell and direct them in the right way. So my niece wanted to go to this party so bad she slipped and told me that the party was called a "NICE BOOTY" party. I never heard of such, but that's what she said. She went on to tell me they (the boys) would be looking for shaped BOOTIES. Well, at that time, I WAS THE BOSS, and I said NO! I don't want you to go to a party like that! "Oh please, Auntie," she said, "everybody at school keep talking about how fun the party is going to be, and I want to go! Please, Auntie, please?" I said again, "NO!" So she did not go, and the next morning, THAT PARTY WAS ON THE FRONT PAGE OF A NEWSPAPER (WHAT A MESS) and on the news all day. I remember the news showed a tennis shoe on the driveway where that party was held. Someone did a drive-by shooting, and of course, they didn't know who! My niece came from school saying, "OH, Auntie, thank you for not letting me go to that party! A lot of teenagers got hit by some of the bullets, and one boy died." I CALLED THOSE BULLETS YES BULLETS because the teens that were there got a *YES* from their parents, and GOD BLESS the boy that got hit. All our hearts were so sad. The teens at school were heartbroken over the loss of their friend they were used to seeing every day; it was awful. BUT my niece found out *NO* is not such an ugly bad word after all; she was thankful for the word *NO*. Ladies, as females, we use the word *YES* more than the males use it. PAY ATTENTION.

Smart or Dumb?
(Choose One!)

Relationship with GOD is special: If your guy is faking, he could block your blessings. Ladies so many guys say I will make you love me.

Male: You love me, baby?

Female: Oh yes. Do you love me?

Male: What do you think? Can't you tell?

Now why didn't he just say *YES*? 'Cause, ladies, we melt with a *yes* and *oh* if he replies with a sexy *yes*. OH, that's it! HE gets our body, car, money, and a hot meal, just with that one *yes*. Are we weak for love or attention, wanting to be needed, or what, ladies? We are needed; first of all you need you, then we need each other to talk and cry together so we can come to terms and get ideas and answers about why we think were not good enough to have the kind of life we want with or without a man. Ladies, we have to know we can't buy love; once you start paying for love and attention, you will have to keep doing it over and over and over. We can't live a happy life like that! Whoever we pay to be with us, ladies, HE or SHE won't respect us or care about us, and when it's all said and done, they won't be there in the end. You don't buy friends either; they will drain you dry and be laughing at you all the time.

We can tell when someone really wants to be around us. Your soul is happy and warm. You will feel the joy of having a friendship. You'll not feel contented and wonderful if you're not liked or loved by friends; everyone wants and needs a friend. And, ladies, when you're the only one that works and works and gives and gives, that's not the way GOD said for men to be. GOD said if man won't work, then man won't eat. We love being with a man because he enjoys coming where you are. We must not chase a man! And when you find him, he will ask how much money you have and how much can you let him have? Some of us, ladies, give up every penny we have just so he will stay around you. And usually he's waiting for the chance to hurry and get to the other lady's house. The song says "you can't hurry love." My song is "don't buy love, you won't get what you paid for!"

Ladies, if he's not spending, don't you spend either; you'll be jumping the gun, and that's no fun. We won't get a wedding day if he sees and thinks were dumb. So stay on top of your thoughts and your actions when you're around him or on the phone with him. And please, ladies, we can't sound anxious when were on the phone either! Gotta make him sweat a little; a man loves what he works for and treasures it for years, so it will be worth your time and mind to stand a different ground for once and stay busy working on you while he wonders about you from a distance. You have to watch him anyway! Don't pay him, WATCH HIM! Ladies, you know everything you want in this life, and you know a BROKE man is not our answer!

We don't mind if he works as a garbage man; that money is still green, and it pays the bills. A garbage worker is wonderful; after all, he cleans himself up. We will welcome them in as long as there is no garbage in his heart; we will take chances on them. I know a lot of times we hated those times when we took that chance 'cause we have a knack to forgive and put up with a lot of his junk they put in our lives. Most of us, ladies, go the long mile; sometimes it works out, and most of the time, it won't. That's why you have to get you going right, make your money, and keep your money until the time is right for you to share your life with him. And you know when that time is, right? After you have watched him! AND you'll know he will work to give his wife money. Is a love gesture? YOU KNOW he will fix things around the house. YOU KNOW he will and can cook, wash clothes, and shop just in case you can't or are too tired when you get home. WATCH and make sure he's good to his mother, that's important! REMEMBER THAT. And most of all, make sure he has a good relationship with GOD. If he's a fake, he will block your blessings. Ladies, so many of us end up with the blessing blockers; that's what I call a bad case of the BB's. So what if we have a baby alone, it's better than having a bad case of BB's. Now don't you agree? Just think about it deep for a while: the baby needs MILK, and he needs BEER. You need a CAR, and he needs a BUS PASS. YOU need some new HAIR, and he needs a HAIRCUT. YOU need a WASHER and DRYER, and he needs CABLE TV. YOU need NEW MAKEUP, and he needs a WRISTWATCH. Because he still can't give you the time of day! So, ladies, to say this is to say that you need to pay yourself first; you have plenty of time to give to him. Right now get up to where you need to be, in a peaceful nice position and kick back and just WATCH!

Stick to the Rules

Listen up, ladies. A lot of times *YES* does not get him the right girl or woman either. That's why if you find a guy with a line full of *yes's* and proves the *yes* word to you, GRAB HIM; he's one in a million. Ladies, we have got to stick to our guns! That means the *NO* word until we see all the *yes's* he pours out. That's why *NO* is good; it keeps us more focused on us. WE have to remember things in our minds and in our hearts. Like, what do I want to be? How will I be all I can be? What is most important about me? Where do I see myself in the next five years? Have I found my purpose yet because I have to find it? Can I set up a foundation for later in life in case I get to the *YES* word too fast? Do I have my backup ready? What makes me smart? What makes me dumb? Ladies, the only answer to most of this is GOD keeps me smart and sex will make me dumb. IF we are not married, we need to watch that sex; it has such a hold on us, ladies, sometimes. Most of the time, we can't think what makes us smart or dumb when that *sex* word is floating around, seems nothing else counts; we all have been like that, ladies. That's why we have to change the way we think. Don't take this ugly! SEX is and can be beautiful; GOD put males and females in this world so everything he made is good. But we make *male and female* not good when we don't allow the RULES to put us together with our sex. The RULES are in the BIBLE; in case you're wondering, WHAT RULES?

THAT'S THE BREAK'S

When your man's found another, that leaves you out. That's the breaks, that's the breaks. But YOU found a man that's RICH, so SHOUT, "That's the breaks, that's the breaks!"

Understand this, ladies, we can play tit for tat if we want to, BUT what fun is that? Trying to keep up with someone—mainly your man, her man, his man—when he is untrue (I like to call it).to us? We want to be untrue to him, and that only hurts us because we will take chances to be with someone we don't even know and usually that means having sex. I knew a girl once when I lived in California, and she lived down the block from me. Well, she had sex with so many guys, and she was going to have a baby. The bigger she got, the more you would hear her say, "I DON'T KNOW WHO! I DON'T KNOW WHO!" She was so sad and unhappy with her life, and she had other children, real cute kids, but she stayed high a lot. When we humans are high, our minds are taken over by you-know-who and his demons; once our minds are not focused, our bodies have no say so at all. That's why GOD warns us to stay away from STRONG DRINK, but we don't listen, and then we end up in jail or hospital or the morgue or with a baby, like my girl GALE, who lived down the street. And then that devil and his demons are laughing at us. Ladies, you will be so mad and feel bad the next day, if you make it to the next day. IF your man does it, let him suffer for that. Don't put your smart self out there and then worry all week long if he had germs. YES, he had germs, and they weren't yours, BUT now they are! You don't know where this guy has been 'cause you don't know him anyway! So, ladies, tit for tat. You have to tell the devil "I PASS." Those are his games anyway. Without GOD, we can't keep up with nothing. No man is worth chasing around; you will lose your self-respect if you chase and follow him around especially if he does not want us with him. Ladies, that's degrading and that makes all of us look so small-minded; his actions are telling you NO! And if you don't know that yet, you will find out, for some of us, the hard way, and the rest of us, by the hair of our CHINNY CHIN CHIN. And always remember whatever he, she, or it puts out, IT'S RIGHT BACK ATCHA. So, ladies, if you're on the bad couch, this is a good time to get up!

RING, RING.

Wake-up call!

Lies, Lies, No-ho More Lies

Ladies, when we pretend we know enough about love, life, and liberty and the time comes to prove ourselves to our peers, our children, our husbands, our families, and last of all, ourselves, a lot of us calm down and can't take the outcome of our lies or the chances we took to get into the position to start the lies. See, lies are not real, so that means the person telling the lies, well, they're not real. To say this, looking back at a very shocking moment in my younger days, I was working in a convalescent hospital, and I worked the graveyard shift most of the time back then. But I would work a lot of "WHERE I WAS NEEDED" shifts also.

So I worked a week of day shifts, and a woman passed through my life as a charge nurse. Well, she was a registered nurse; they make big money because they're licensed. They pass out medication to patients, give shots, and do all the legal treatments in a hospital. Now I was just a nursing assistant, trained with a certificate; we do all the work but make less money. Now this charge nurse surely gives out the orders to the little people like me that did all the hard dirty work, but I did what I was told. And I had respect for my elders, and I still do. And as the head nurse, she, for some strange, strange reason, told the director that I called her and said that he had better get his shit together. And what I called in for was my paycheck. See, it was my day off, so I wanted to pick my check up. When I called to see if the checks were in from payroll, she answered the phone on that day; she knew exactly who I was, and she spoke real nice to me.

She said, "Hold on. I will transfer you to the director's office." It took a little while before he picked up the extension. I waited, of course, because I wanted to get my check, and all of the sudden, he picked the extension up and yelled in my ear. "You can pick up your check and consider yourself without a job here anymore." I wanted to speak, but he hung up in my face. Now why did such a lady with freckles all over her face with red short hair tell and make up such a lie on me like that? I just wonder what hate was in her heart for me and why. What could she gain from this lie? I was a real good worker and always kept her shift that she was in charge of running smoothly.

So why me? I was so shocked that she would lie like that. Especially at her age. But I know some answers now. My GOD, our GOD, says jealousy is crueler than a grave, and they talked about him, spat on him, told lies on him, and more things than I could ever take. GOD is a good GOD, and I know now that he died for me and you, for us, (I did not always know that). And GOD said, "No weapon formed against me shall prosper," and she formed a weapon with her lying tongue against me. But GOD sits high and looks low, and I know he saw what that so-called nurse did. GOD let me know in his word, he said, "I'll fight your battle if you keep still." And I was very angry at that nurse, I don't know if I would have hit her if I saw her or what! But I remember I really wanted her to talk to me face-to-face and tell me why she MADE IT UP, and I mean MADE UP that lie like that! WHY? I think I would have felt a little better about losing my job if she could have been made to tell me WHY? As I'm thinking deeply about this, I should have called the police on her; I'm sorry I didn't ! But one thing I know is, "when you dig a ditch, dig two because you will be falling in the same ditch you dug for me." That's why I had to let GOD fight that battle for me. I WANTED TO WIN! So with that, I can exhale and go forward. HALLELUJAH! I'VE GOT THE VICTOR—VICTOR—VICTORY!

GOSSIP

Ladies, I think when we gossip, we are meaning to do one another harm. Not too often will we gossip and say something good about each other. I guess if we say good things about each other, it would not be gossip, which means, not interesting, not fun, do you see yourself talking about "Girl, she is so together. I hope she gets to have the guy of her dreams. She really needs for that to happen for her!" AND "I really want her to get that job I wanted, she surely qualifies better than me" THOUGHT? IF YOU CAN'T SAY SOMETHING GOOD, DON'T SAY NOTHING AT ALL! You have heard that saying before, haven't you? Well, we never listened or paid any attention to the meaning, did we? WRONG! You know we will not stick to that saying, but ladies, we should. We have to stop the gossip! The BIBLE calls it "being a busybody." I call it BACKBITING. What do you call it? I hope you have a real bad name for it so we can stop it and pass it on that. "YOU'LL NEVER GET TO HEAVEN IF YOU BREAK MY HEART!

SO BE VERY CAREFUL NOT TO!" And that is what gossip is; it's a heartbreaker. When we find out someone, family, friend, or foe, has said something about us that is bad and hateful, our heart breaks. Then next usually comes the anger, then usually, and most certainly, the fights! Ladies, let it start with you. Let it start with me to change the way we talk, walk, and wink. We all have good and bad feelings; why let your brother or sister feel the way YOU hate to feel by saying something about them when their back is turned? GOD says, "Pull your brother to the side." Then you can get it all out but in a peaceful way. We will feel so much better with the peace. I have a stepsister who won't speak to me right today; I don't know why, but whenever she gets it all out, I will be ready, willing and able to make things better between us. And whatever she is angry with me about, I want to hug and kiss her then talk about whatever it is so this won't happen again and keep us apart or out of heaven! Ladies, when we can't and don't mend our hearts with each other, it's that ugly,

ugly PRIDE! Just in case you did not know, GOD hates pride! That's how the devil got thrown out of heaven! So everyone needs to solve their problems while they can; don't get caught with your work undone. Every dot has to be over the *i*, and every *t* has to be crossed; we won't get it any other way! We have to be in ORDER, GOT THAT?

YOUR TREASURES

Ladies, we can't keep getting on any man's bed; we have to stop! And if you are not, don't start. YES, some of us get in bed with any man. When we do that, we are making ourselves look dumber than a person that has been in the second grade for ten years. WE must keep some pride here, ladies. When you go to bed with a person that you don't know (and if you give them your body knowing you don't know them), they usually never call you again or come back in your life at all. You have totally disrespected yourself. How small are you thinking? How smart are you? When you do those kind of things and you're an adult, that makes you pretty dumb now, doesn't it?

God gave women the greatest treasure there is. We possess jewels, pearls, rubies, diamonds, emeralds, and topaz. We possess everything; our treasures that came straight from God—all those wonderful jewels we have in our bodies—but we don't treasure them at all. Just give us a drink or something to smoke or something to eat, and we give our precious jewels away at the drop of a hat. Isn't that sad, ladies? And then we look at the next days, months, or years, and no one is there but you—without your treasures. They haven't been stolen; you gave them away, yes.

The treasure of your body, the treasure of your mind, the treasure of your self-respect, the treasure of your pride, the treasures of your dignity, and most important of all, the treasures of your heart—those are treasures God gave you; those are treasures GOD gave me! Those are treasures God gave us to keep safe and precious until he sends us a husband to give the key to; NOW that opens the treasure chest of our hearts. Ladies, this key is the key to our souls. This key is so very important; don't just give it to anyone. It has access to so many important doors.

See, ladies, a key gives anyone access to certain things, to certain places. Without a key, you just can't get in, not the right way; without a key, you can break in or enter inside without permission. Then you will be in trouble, usually with the law or with GOD. So a key is very important to have because you have permission when you have a key. This is why God says he has the key to the kingdom. He is letting us know that he has the key, and we can enter heaven because he has given us permission, and he can give us permission because he has the key. See, whoever has the key is in charge, and you have the keys to your treasures; so you're in charge of yourself. You got that, ladies? YOU'RE IN CHARGE! You are the one that can get grand viva!

GRAND VIVA! That's high steppin', and that's you! So get into your position, ladies, and always stay there. Now without the key to our treasure chests, ladies, nothing comes forth in the human race. What you have is royal and worth more than money, cars, homes, food, drinks, and the lottery. Yes, ladies, watch over your treasures. Please realize what you have possession of because God made us so special; we can't take this lightly. Concentrate, ladies, as I continue on the subject of our treasures. My older sister's baby son once had a dog; we called her Angel. She was the breed of Afghan.

And the Afghan dogs, well, the female Afghans are very, very proud dogs, in case you didn't know. Well, Angel was a beautiful light brown-and-gold-colored dog; she was beautiful, sophisticated, and lovely. And you could look at her and tell she knew it. She sat so proud with her head up in an abundance of pride; that's all you would see. That is the only dog I can say that I loved. If I was sitting in the living room or on the front porch, she would look at me with her beautiful brown eyes and then she would sit at my feet. She always made me feel like I had the female pride when she would sit with such sophistication and control. I always paid attention to that! And I thought how I need to feel like that every day. It had to be a good feeling because it looked so good!

Then later in the year, Angel started sneaking down the alley or next door where the other dogs were. And she ended up having two different leaders of puppies. Now she had the puppies alone, fed them alone, and raised them alone. No daddies, no child support, no love for her or the puppies. Now that's what the dogs do, right? All they need is the male puppy for mating, and the male dog has pretty much done his job as a male dog, or shall I say a male dad. Then I look at us, human women. We get with some guy; he's maybe cute (I say maybe because the ugly men have three or four women in this day and time). But we may date him once or twice. Sometimes, we don't date at all; we go straight to bed and give our treasures away like we are passing out luncheon meat sandwiches.

"YOU KNOW, IT'S NO BIG DEAL AT ALL." Then we usually come with child, left alone to have the baby alone. No daddy, no father, and no man in the household to help rule and teach the children and direct them in the way they should go. Only the female is there alone with her children. And just as the dog Angel, LEFT WITH HER PUPPIES! My point is, ladies, we are not treated any different from Angel, THE DOG! WE'RE HUMAN! WE'RE HUMAN! WE'RE HUMAN! WHAT IS WRONG WITH THIS PICTURE? Ladies, we have got to make things change for each other.

We won't go to meetings and vote for a change, but we have got to think better, speak differently, and act more like we want better for ourselves and for our children to help our families to become better people in society. Ladies, let it start with you and me. We must carry ourselves differently, with respect and dignity. Do we know what dignity is? It is something that we really do want and need, and you will like it. (IT'S GOOD GIRL!) Dignity is good. It feels good. And we need it so others will know what we are about—ladies. We are not a luncheon meat sandwich! We are women. We are queens made from the HIGH CALLING OF GOD to bring forth human life from beautiful treasures that were given to us by GOD. So we have to keep ourselves pretty and sweet as sugar at all times so no one ever again will take us or call us a sandwich. We can and we will change that image!

WE will let the men know that our price is far beyond RUBIES, just like the Bible says. WE are bought with a high price—THE BLOOD OF JESUS. Thus, we don't come cheap. And if he didn't know that, it's time we, ladies, speak up and tell the world who and what we are. And the next time he wants to talk about your treasure chest, then you just watch what he does in his "going" and in his "coming." Then your heart will know if he's worthy of THE KEY. (DID WE GET THAT, ladies?) IT'S TIME TO JUST SIT BACK AND WATCH HIM! Ladies, try to feel what I'm saying right here NOW. While watching him, we want to see and really pay attention to the following: (1) where he lives; can you see yourself living there? (2) does he have a television? (3) a watch on his wrist? IF not, remember he can't give you the time of day. He only has one thing to offer you that won't cost him a dime. OH, and ladies, does he have his own cell phone? Or will he want you to get him one, on your bill, in your name? So far, ladies, if there are none of these things happening as you're watching him, then it's nine times out of ten he does not have a JOB! OK!

Now some of us don't care if he works or not; we think we've got it. And if you think you can work and he doesn't have to, you are messing with GOD'S plan. Ladies, if he's healthy, you are making him so weak by not insisting that he bring his income in the household. Now if he doesn't work for his own self, probably he won't work for you either. If he can't buy himself a car, then guess what, he won't be buying you one. Ladies, if he has his own car when you met him, then keep an eye on him quietly. Pay attention to how his car looks.

Is it clean in and out? Most good men like their car shining, most men that is. Usually a man's car is his "pride and joy." Their car always impresses them. You can usually know what a man is really all about if you see his car and his shoes; most of the time, not all the time. Pay attention, okay! Listen up! Like I said before, if he has a mother, well, just really, really watch how he treats her. If he loves and adores her, you're in luck! GRAB HIM! He most likely will adore and love you. IF he treats his mother bad (by being mean and disrespectful and has a filthy mouth), RUN the other way as fast as you can; he will not make you happy. Ladies, LISTEN. Now some of us find a good man through GOD sending them our way. And we have had faith that GOD will give us the desire in our hearts like how he told us in his word; then we get our desire, but we weaken him by not letting him be all the man he can be. Sometimes we are so busy helping him, we ruin him. We ALLOW him NOT to be the man GOD told him to be—that is, the head of his household; the head of the house is supposed to provide! He is ordered to keep a roof over his family's head, put food on the table, and clothes on their backs. We, ladies, step in his shoes and go to work, pay the bills, and provide the food, etc. Ladies, we are not letting him bloom into the man GOD meant for him to be. He can't grow if we're doing his JOB for him. STOP IT, ladies! That makes you a BB. Don't block him anymore; you must let him take care of you. Let him rescue you and the family first, then, ladies, you can rescue him right back! But move out of the way; let him work! That's what GOD meant for him to do. When GOD made him, THAT WAS GOOD!

When GOD made Adam, he meant for him to do the same thing—to take care of Eve. But she wanted to run the show, so she picked the apple and fed it to Adam. She made him weak; that took his manhood before he could even get into the world good. So, ladies, LET GO AND LET GOD! He makes no mistakes, no mistakes! Ladies, MOVE! Just sit down, let him do it, he will! Ladies, the word says GOD made man in his own image, so man is very, very important here on earth. HE WAS MADE IN THE IMAGE OF GOD, and he made man good because he is good.

OUR men are good, and we will always be humble to the will of GOD for making man. They are the most important being on earth because GOD made and gave them authority to BE THE HEAD AND RUN THE WORLD, DECENT AND IN ORDER. Ladies, my view is, man has gotten out of order because he stopped doing what GOD said to do. And GOD gave man directions how to run the world, but being in the flesh, man did things his own way, and now everyone is looking for the new president to put HUMPTY DUMPTY back together again! But men were all good in the beginning, and we have to believe there are more good men left, and they will step up to the plate before it's too late.

So to all of the ladies who read this book, know that you are charged to spread the word to others, and to pray for our men in the world; that includes SMALL MEN, TALL MEN, GOOD MEN, RICH MEN, POOR MEN,

WHITE MEN, BLACK MEN, GREEN MEN, YELLOW MEN, and PURPLE MEN TO become more GODLY MEN and BE ABOUT THEIR FATHER'S BUSINESS. And our problem with all men as head of the household and as leaders of this wonderful world will go away. They MUST get on the WINNING side so they can always win. And we all know, ladies, who wins battles! When our men wake up, they will, and they can make this world better. That's why we, ladies, have to stick together so all our men will work together. And that's the way GOD wants it. HE WOULDN'T HAVE IT ANY OTHER WAY! GOT THAT!

Hungry

When I was a child, we never had much to eat around our house. I remember the time when luncheon meat or a hot dog was a luxury meal. My memory takes me back when my sisters and I would enjoy having a Miracle Whip sandwich with only the mayo on two pieces of bread, no meat in between. I guess there was no money to buy any, so we loved and enjoyed the mayo sandwich; they were so good. As I remembered, we never cared about having any meat in the bread. If we did, it was fine; if we did not, it was good. God let us enjoy a mayo sandwich so well that we didn't even think about being poor.

We were just hungry for that particular mayo sandwich. As I got older, I got hungry for a different type of sandwich. As a teenager, my hunger was for new clothes and going to parties because the boys would surely be at the parties. And I was hungry for boys to look at me (if he was cute and could dance good), so I would always try to find out where all the parties were. Back in those days, you did not need an invitation per se. And my girlfriends and I would walk to all the parties we could, even in the snow. The cold did not bother us at all. We knew when we got to the party we would forget about being cold. Then I got hungry for other bigger and better things, and even my thoughts were different.

My thoughts and hunger were of entertainment; this hunger had me starving, yet the hunger had my full attention, and I had to find out where to sit down and eat. All the time, it was in my own backyard, RIGHT at my school. It got so that I wanted more parts in the plays at school. There never were enough plays to be in for me. I loved it so much when we did *The Unsinkable Molly Brown* show because it had singing and dancing in it, and I was good at both. OH, and that's when my big sister bought me my first pair of high heels; they were patent leather on one side, and the other side of the shoe was leather, and I had on a pair of RED FOX STOCKINGS.

I thought I was a real star for the two nights we gave the performances. But now, I sing in the shower and direct plays from my chair most of the time. I have a real good girlfriend. I call her my right-hand man; her name is Marie, but calling her my right-hand man is our little giggle stuff she and I do sometimes. She helps me produce all the plays; she keeps the children in line especially right before a performance. I love her so much; she keeps the costumes in order and does so many other wonderful things as my sister. My older sisters always help me with any production with their ideas, their wisdom, and most of all, their love and patience. I appreciate all of them, and I don't take their love for me lightly. And I truly know I'm blessed to still have them around at this time in my life.

Now that I'm older, I hunger for more important things, and, ladies, we all have to and need to change some of our hunger habits. We have to find our purpose in this life, and if you have not found it, do not stop looking because God did not make you and put you here on this earth for nothing! That's not the way he works. When you do find your purpose, you will help the world be a better place to live. And you will love yourself better; then you will get hungry for bigger and better ways and means to go after the real you, and the better part of your life is just getting started. Ladies, we can get hungry for better health; that's important. Without that, our dreams will fade, so keep looking up!

OH! We really need to be hungry for wealth; our country is letting us know that. And please get hungry for success, and we ALL need to be hungry for FAITH. Now, ladies, we have to know ourselves so we can know what we want; especially when we get hungry, we must know what to eat good out of this life. While we are getting, get this: Ladies are NO longer hungry for the blues. Ladies, a little hunger for attention, never hurt anyone. Sometimes I get real, real hungry for my mother. Is there anyone out there with me on that one? NOW we have a real bad hunger for complete happiness. Yes, GOD said we can have that completeness of anything we ask for as long as we love and obey his laws and put no one and nothing before him.

AND as your sister, I proudly stand and proclaim that, "We are hungry for a HIGH STATUS in life and with GOD. WE are hungry for that FOUNDATION we talked about early in the book." OH, ladies! PLEASE get HUNGRY for that PEACE OF MIND we want and need. GO ahead and get hungry for LOVE. Now there's a song that says, "LOOKIN' FOR LOVE IN ALL THE WRONG PLACES." Make sure we HUNGER for GOD'S LOVE FIRST so he will bless us with THE TRUE LOVE WE DESERVE HERE ON EARTH! AND YES, YES, YES, ladies. WE have to be HUNGRY FOR THE TRUTH. WITH THE TRUTH, WE can HUNGER TO BE, AND WILL BE FREE! Most of all, of these to get,

GET hungry for the food that comes from the Bible, and this counts more than the sun itself. WE HAVE TO GET HUNGRY FOR THE WORD.

Once we are full of that food, we will be happy and contented. Now we won't be happy and contented until we are full of the word because this is the main course of the meal, and we always eat the main meal. RIGHT? GOD said, "HUNGER NO MORE!" There are so many things in this day and time, ladies, that we can get hungry for; that will do us a lot of good. IF we are NOT happy with all of the GOOD hunger we have, THE ENEMY has plenty of mess the human race hungers for. HERE WE GO! Drugs, sex, jail, liquor, guns, dagger, and DANGER with CARS; that's why they HIJACK CARS! And sometimes they'll hurt us if we don't give our cars to them. There is even a hunger for KILLING and STEALING—hunger for a MAN, sometimes ANY MAN! LETTING NOTHING stop us from having a MEAL LIKE HIM!

Then when we get with that MEAL WE JUST HAD TO HAVE, and we find out he's dangerous and has a hunger for KILLING, so guess where we'd end up? There are so many different kinds of hunger, so ladies, we must watch our cravings. But we don't care about any hunger the enemy has, now do we? NO! Our ULTIMATE HUNGER IS FOR HEAVEN! IF you have ever been starving for anything really bad, please GET HUNGRY FOR HEAVEN. If we are hungry for this BEAUTIFUL PLACE BAD enough, we will do what GOD says to make it in! SOMEONE SAID, "BY ANY MEANS NECESSARY," so let's PRESS TOWARD THE MARK OF THE HIGH CALLING OF GOD! And, ladies, we will never be HUNGRY ever again. AND THAT'S REAL!

THIS COMPLETES THE FIRST PART OF MY BOOK! GET READY FOR PART 2. SISTERS, WE'RE WONDERFUL!

Part II

DANCING

Guess what, dancing is for women! Dancing is so wonderful; it's like floating in the air that lets us feel free, especially if you can waltz wearing one of those long beautiful gowns on. Oh, ladies, just close your eyes and picture yourself waltzing around a dance floor, beautiful, light, smelling good with a real expensive cologne on, a handsome tall man leading you around and around in total freedom. Ladies, does that sound like something you would order if you could? Well, I would at least once in my lifetime; I still might. I'm not finished yet. MY older sisters always went to the dances when they were teenagers, so you know I had to do the same thing.

I liked to dance with guys that are tall, neat, and smells good. One of the bad memories I have is about a slow dance. I was dancing with a boy in junior high school (we had a party one afternoon), and he was just moving his feet in one small circle and breathing real loud. And his hot stinky breath was on my shoulder and in my ear; this was full of torture for me, and I said, "I have to go to the restroom." Seems that song was never going to end (smile). I couldn't take it anymore; that breathing was sick! A bad dance has its memories. THERE'S A SONG CALLED "DON'T MESS WITH BILL." My saying was "DON'T MESS WITH BREATH!"

There were a few good dancers in junior high school. We used to have a ninth-grade dance on Friday mornings, and Bobby Jones, Larry, and Joseph Thomas were about the best ones to dance with. All the girls would stay away from the guys with bad breath. The good thing is I have had more good dances than I ever could dream of. My first good dance was in the third grade. At the city auditorium, we had to have a boy partner, and you were picked by the gym teacher. Well, I was picked from our class, and we did the IRISH JIG. And it was an honor if you danced in the school festival because all dancers came from all over, so we got to meet other kids. My next good dance was at the Color Day breakfast dance at my high school. I was in the tenth grade, and I got to sing a solo and dance that time; so that was a treat! And later, I found out I was in the rocky mountain newspaper singing; I think I had about five or six newspapers. I thought it was a pretty cute picture! I was so proud.

Then as I got older and could go out to different nightclubs and dance, I met THE MR. MOZEE. He was one of the best dancers I ever danced with; that's probably what made me marry him. Plus I was still dumb and blind; GOD was talking to me, but I was not listening. WE would dance everywhere we went, and people would watch us dance around the floor. It was so nice I thought I was a queen for a night! (Smile.) But those days are gone; you can't get it back. NOW, I have to cut me a little step for the Lord, not only 'cause we were asked to, but because I personally think dancing for GOD is also a gift.

But we were at a musical at my church. It was real good; I loved it. I laughed with my sister that night; we were so happy trying to dance with each other. Please know that dancing makes you so happy, carefree, strong, popular, and very womanish if you're in a nice atmosphere. With a candle lit and with the right dancer, we can feel JUST WONDERFUL AND SIMPLY MARVELOUS, DARLING! And, ladies, we all need a dancing good time in this life, so press your way and get yourself a dance! DANCING IS GREAT; DANCING IS GOOD. TRY IT. YOU'LL LIKE IT. YOU CAN BE UNDERSTOOD! AND THAT'S REAL TOO!

The father of my grandsons, I only wish he would wake up and know that GOD has charged him to be the head and take care of his family and to be the main provider of his household (1 Timothy 5:8). IF YOU WILL, GOD does not want him to sit back and watch his wife go to work and only help out now and then. The enemy has him fooled. MAYBE he will one day have a big popular church; I'm not saying he doesn't have the will to be a big-shot preacher. But when there's a lazy demon present some of us have been carrying around for years and can't see that the enemy has had people like that for a long, long time, that blocks us from being all we can be. When the lazy demon is present, I pray that one day soon we will step back and see that demon, get rid of it, and send it back to the pits of hell where it came from. If we don't step back, ladies, we won't be able to see through the forest because of the trees (if you will). WE can't see through the forest when are in the middle! We have to step back and LOOK! I only want my son-in-law, my daughter, and any other young couples with children to rise, be well-off, and find that FOUNDATION we were talking about in the book.

Ladies, we can change our lives and make them MO' BETTER! I love my kids and their mates; mothers just want things in life better for her loving children. I only wanted more for my children, like any mother would! If I were in control, she would be married to GOD and GOD only (he is a GOD of high standards) to make sure she would never want for nothing that was out of her reach or suffer in any way or do without as an adult. The children have already done without as children, and I prayed for a better, softer life for all my babies; I always told her she was special, and she needed to be very careful because she is special, which meant WATCH WHO YOU KEEP COMPANY WITH.

Be careful of your surroundings, and be picky of WHO YOU CHOOSE to spend the rest of your life with; the enemy will put his people in our path to keep us quiet so that we won't do the work we were put here to do. I think the enemy will send blockers when any of GOD'S children are ESPECIALLY chosen to be sent out to do his will in the world. He will hide you in a little room and call it your church and give you a title of the first lady of GOD so you won't see the real plan he has for you. He keeps us where we were NOT REALLY called to work for GOD. My daughter is a public person; the public pays attention when she is out there speaking or when she prays or when she is using her healing hands God gave her. That's why the enemy has her hidden. He knows she can do great work in the public for GOD, so he hides her, and she allows it.

But please know, ladies, GOD is not a hidden GOD. He said every man will know him and be given a chance to accept him. So, ladies, we can't hide GOD in a small corner and think we are pleasing him; your fruit will not show up on your tree or in your life. Others will see your branches are EMPTY, and they will FLEE from you. I wanted my kind of control to spell love to my daughter, not sickness and HATE. Here I'm alive and well, and she hardly ever calls me. I wish my mother would have lived this long for me to be around. She comes by once in a while, and all she thinks of me is I want control of her or her life. I would never step on my own baby. I would never step on anyone's baby; the enemy has her heart thinking that.

But GOD warned us about the signs, and I know I love my little girl, and she is special; that enemy thinks he had her special in his own way. NOW ISN'T THAT A LOU LOU? NO ONE CAN OUTTHINK GOD! AND WE CAN'T STOP HIS PROGRAM! HE WILL USE WHO AND WHAT HE WANTS, AND THAT'S REAL! But I'm stuck like glue to my daughter because I have all THIS love for her. AND I KNOW LOVE STICKS! YET in my heart and my older sisters' hearts, we are still hurt by my mother leaving us so very young. That's why we wanted better for our children, but we made it. By God's grace and mercy, surely GOODNESS and MERCY shall follow me. (I HAVE TO KEEP SAYING THAT TO MAKE SURE THEY ARE WITH ME.) We could have turned out in so many ugly ways; we are thankful. We came through okay with wisdom, knowledge, and understanding. Then God came through with his warm love that we didn't get from our mother or father. All we can say good is they were married when they made the three sisters. So we were not born bastards! And that's all I have to say about that!

Out of the Tunnel

Back in those days, my second sister told my mother she wanted to be a doctor, and she remembers our mother replying, "THEY don't let black people be doctors." Now why did she not encourage my sister? (THAT REPLY WAS NOT HEALTHY, MAMA!) Back in those days, being of dark skin was not good. You just could not go to college and be what you wanted to be. (But you sure can now!) We used to be so ashamed of where we lived, being broke, and having nothing. I was so ashamed if kids knew my mother died. I just did not want them to know because it was such a bad feeling for me to know I didn't have a mother at home, and I didn't want the other children to know I was going home with no mother there.

As a teenager, I was embarrassed to let my boyfriend know my mother died. He found out, but he liked me anyway. And I ended up marrying him years later. But I had to come out of that tunnel because it was too dark. And I could not see my way with a liquor bottle blocking my happiness, my future, and my peace. I came from a home as a child that didn't have much peace in it. Maybe that's why I love the peace I have now, and I won't give it up for nothing or anybody. When we were little girls, we were real skinny, no weight problem at all, never had any food at all until Fridays when the hell raiser got paid.

We had lots of mayo and bread sandwiches; luncheon meat was like a T-bone steak of today. Now we have plenty of food to eat, and I'm sure we have a weight problem because we make sure we are not like we were coming up hungry and poor with hardly any food at all. So we are getting a grip on this eating habit; we're learning to eat healthy now. I think if we would have been taught as young girls to eat healthy, it would be that way today with us, and we wouldn't have to train ourselves at this age to eat healthy. It's hard too! And we're all good cooks; our mother was a real good cook. She would make cakes from scratch (pies); anything she cooked was good, and for some reason, all of us girls cook a lot like her. That's funny, though, because she never sat down and taught us word for word; I think we automatically got it from her.

Work Harder

My ladies, we, as women, realize there is always work to do at home, at work, at church, and really in our community. I say we need to go to a high level of awareness and really find out what we are able to give of ourselves and get it out directly in the lives and laps of others. I know this will reflect on any transformation that we have happening and bubbling inside of us. If our hearts are in the right place, we can surely be likely to accomplish all that we set out to do now and, at least, for the rest of this year. But whatever is on our hearts, we must put our foot down and work harder at it. Ladies, a little work has never hurt anyone. Please know a little sweat won't offend me. Ladies, I found out in my old age, sweat is real, real good for me and you!

We need to sweat every day, ladies, in the transformation of different levels of life. When I say different levels, I mean we can be at a lower level and move up (which is good) or we can be at a higher level and move down (which we should not want to do). Growing can develop excellent skills when our minds are focused on being more of a woman of God or bringing up our skills to a higher level—may it be higher learning, self-control, or shopping and eating with good control. Learning to cook with the healthy transformation process of thinking also involves saying, "I don't want it if it's not good for my body. And I need it to be good for my mind also."

Ladies, as for myself, I really want to invent a healthy community to be in at all times for myself and others around me. If no one is around me, then I want to work hard alone. Ladies, we can make conscious decisions so that we can be the BEST we can be. And we all really do need to be the BEST we can be! We can use our minds to go forward with new ways and means and making things mo' better for us and people around us. Sometimes it's hard work because we are so programmed to eating or thinking and speaking in a certain way that our thinking is sometimes STUCK. They call it STUCK ON STUPID. Here we GO. (Can't stop drinking liquor even if your doctor says so). STUCK, HUH? Can't put the cake down even if you're told you could live ten extra years? STUCK!

Then we are STUCK on DOPE. And all your money goes up in smoke, and then you're mad at yourself. You hate her or him that is in the mirror; can't sleep, can't eat, that's STUCK, ladies. Stuck! Then the sad, sad part is when we get so out there and stuck and can't get back. We often then find ourselves STUCK on not wanting to learn more about the world, about God, or about you! There is so much more about you that is waiting inside to be found. OH, how sad to think that a lot of us, the human race, won't work harder to find more of our selves. We are too lazy to DIG DEEP. and ladies, to find the rest of me takes harder work, so we have to DIG. LADIES, LISTEN UP! Please try not to leave this earth and not bring out the rest of you: I'll say it AGAIN; there is so much more of you to work on in YOU, for YOU, and with YOU! The world will be much happier when we give all we have inside our hearts and souls. Ladies, if we don't work hard as we can on being and bringing out all of the YOU in US, well, we have not completed the circle of the human life. WE ARE INCOMPLETE! What if we get to heaven and God tells us we're INCOMPLETE on earth. If we, ladies, are INCOMPLETE, whose fault will that be? When there are incomplete toys made or incomplete surgery (sometimes when it's not complete), we can send it back in and complete the mission, BUT I kinda think heaven works different on INCOMPLETE souls going up! I don't know, but I don't want to take any chances. I would like for God to say and know I came to heaven complete. It will be our fault only if we aren't COMPLETE!

We must DIG, DIG, DIG, ladies, and find all that we are inside our mind! My pastor always says, "BY THE RENEWING OF YOUR MIND, we will be different." And, ladies, that's where the other work we need to do on ourselves comes in. We have to work more out of our minds, AND you know what they say, ladies, "THE MIND IS A TERRIBLE THING TO WASTE." I say it's a precious part to waste. Ladies, let's be aware that without our MIND, NOTHING WILL MOVE OR WORK that is connected to the human body! So knowing that, we have a head start! Ladies, we have to bring her forth; you will like her! She is the other YOU that will give us completeness; that we must have about YOU, ME, and I. Ladies, it's just mind work that we have taken with us everywhere we went.

The older you get, you will work more with your minds but listen up! Don't wait until you get older to start DIGGING DEEP. DO IT NOW! You will DIG up more, and you will enjoy doing it more and more. I kid you not! SO LET'S OPEN OUR MINDS UP, LADIES, AND GO BE ALL WE CAN BE, AND WE WILL NOT STOP UNTIL WE KNOW THAT WE ARE COMPLETE. And we will know because we will feel smart, we will feel bold, we will feel pride, and most of all, we will feel LOVE all over our hearts. And the love will shine on our faces FOR ALL TO SEE! And we can always walk with our heads up. If we're in a wheelchair, we will wheel with our heads up.

Walking and running is wonderful, but it's not everything; our mind is the beginning and the end. LADIES, if you have any kind of handicap and you still have your mind, you must press on with everything you have, and if you need a hand to press on, call on the angels God sent to watch over you a long time ago; we all have them. We just didn't know it. Even when we were children, we had them around. Don't feel bad, ladies. I did not know I had mine either until the broken feelings came and the job went, and the plane did not crash when it was raining and thundering, and I was high in the sky; then before I knew it, that plane was landing safe and on time! Or until the labor pains stopped and I gave birth to three healthy babies. Or until I had no credit and the angels moved this realtor man to keep coming to me, telling me I could buy a house alone with just me and three children. And when I stopped and listened to him after I ran away from him over ten times or more, we had our own house in four months. All I did was "WORK HARD." So, ladies, we have so much on our side, and we will come FORTH!

In This Generation

Here and now! First of all, we, ladies, want to be equal to a man in the baby boomer's generation. A lot of us wanted to have equal pay and equal job status; we wanted to wear steel-toe boots and climb poles and connect cable wires, singing and saying, "I can do it all by myself. I don't need a man. I can do the same thing a man can do!" Don't get this the wrong way, ladies. I love all the ways we women can do, have done, and are doing GREAT things in this world, making things better and showing more wisdom in history of womanhood. But, ladies, we have to face it; we can't do everything a man can do. GOD made us different; we were made from the rib of a man. GOD made two of everything—male and female lions, male and female birds, male and female cows, and so on.

There were two of everything, and they were always male and female. He did not make two female ducks or two male goats; it's always one male and one female. Now if you don't believe that, you need to read; start with the first book of the Bible. BUT GOD ONLY MADE ONE MAN! So he saw man was lonely and made ONE WOMAN, and we all know what her name was. Ladies, we are not made to do all things. A lot of us try to do everything for ourselves, and we make it so hard, or we just mess it up all together (nice try). We want to be something we're not, and a lot of times, that puts us in a place we really don't want to be. We can find ourselves homeless and on drugs; sometimes we find us out there in prostitution, sometimes with a pimp that beats us half to death for not making enough money.

Then sometimes we end up with another woman, knowing GOD hates that, and surely there is no reproduction going on, NO replenishing the earth. Now what if the female bull started mating with the other female bull? Or a male cow started mating with a male cow? OUR FOOD SUPPLY would PERISH, in other words, BE GONE, and the human race would starve to death when the two female cows die and they could not make a baby cow to carry on; the same thing with the two male bulls. They can't make a baby bull, now can they? Maybe they were in love, but they can't do what GOD put them here to do, so the human race is again going to starve and _ _ _! LET'S look at the human race: when old men get old, they get old; when old women get old, they get old.

Now the young men are supposed to reproduce a nice human baby, and men sexing with another man will never make another human being; the same thing with women unless you are willing to be an experiment in a doctor's office. You can't reproduce the way GOD said for you to! I have a lot of gay friends that I love talking to or being around. Sometimes, they are human just like me, and sometimes they are some of the best friends you could have. But my name is not GOD. I did not make the rules for the human race to live by, and GOD said NO! (Sad but it's true!) Ladies, the next problem we have to deal with is we have a man shortage. I say it started with VIETNAM! We lost too many young men then after the war; women's rights started, and we felt we didn't need any man to make it. A lot of us found our independence from being on our own and making up our minds on different situations; some of us loved it, and a lot of us did hate the thought of doing and being alone, so some of us turned to another woman for companionship and affection.

But, ladies, that's not in GOD'S plan. So it has got to go! If this was my plan, I could say, well, if you just have to, BUT this is GOD'S plan and you can NOT! ('Cause you won't make it in the gates, please listen to what GOD says!) Then after the women's rights, our male humans formed GANGS, and all they did and still do is KILL one another, and that made our male count real short! THEN so many went to PRISON and only a few got out. And then after that, we have men with men in and out on the DOWN LOW! And if that devil was able, he would have everybody on that shelf! THEN from there came CRACK AND CRYSTAL METH straight from the pits of HELL! And a lot of our men that are still here (and can be counted and be in a nice, warm, cozy home with a family he could be taking care of) wanted to waste their money and time on DRUGS! And that is not a life. They breathe air, but they don't have a life! GETTING BACK TO OUR GENERATION OF WOMEN, WELL, we want to wear the thong panties for every man we think about or look at, but we don't need to know a thing about him. I know a lady, well, she was a beautiful lady, and she met a guy and smoked crack with him over and over. A baby was made, but she did not know a thing about him. The only thing she had was his first and last name, no background or knowledge about where he came from, just nothing at all, but she had his baby, and that was sad. YOU have to want to be pregnant in 2009; there are so many types of birth control in the world today.

Ladies, we are women doing and making moves in our lives that are NOT smart. Babies having babies is not the thing to do; this is NOT SMART or CUTE. LISTEN UP, ONE BABY IS OK! We all make mistakes, so you can handle that! THEN ANOTHER BABY; NO JOB, NO HUSBAND, NO FATHER for the BABY. IT'S JUST PLAIN DUMB! Ladies, no protection for the BOOTY CALL? WE ARE NOT THINKING! WE'RE BACK TO THE CHOICES! OUR CHOICES ARE OUR DESTINY, REMEMBER? In my time of having babies, it was no fun being alone at home or the hospital! So, ladies, how can we help to get our men back in the ARK of God's WORD? LADIES, LET'S SHOW THE MEN THAT WE CAN CHANGE, AND WE HAVE CHANGED. And we must give up our THONGS BY THE RENEWING OF OUR MIND. TAKE THEM OFF!

Why are we buying and selling more THONGS than BIBLES? NOW WHAT'S UP WITH THAT? And, ladies, we need to also stop the tongue piercing by the RENEWING OF YOUR MIND! Ladies, it's a gesture, and it relates to oral sex. And, ladies, we get the worst part of that! So why even waste your lifestyle being put in a position like that? He won't like or love you any better, especially on the first date; you just blew it girl! It's like being a slave on a sex plantation. I KNOW IT'S THE STYLE, BUT IT'S ALSO A BAD CHOICE! And we'll pay for that BAD CHOICE LATER down the line. And when guys see that in a nightclub, they know just what you are about and what you will do with your tongue, and he won't want you for himself because all his buddies see what we, women with our tongue advertisement, want to say. SIMON IN THE BIBLE SAYS, "THE FINAL CONCLUSION FOR ALL THINGS IS FEAR THE LORD." So fear GOD and start loving yourself better. And, ladies, when you find a quiet moment at home, listen to the song "REASONS," and if you find yourself in there, find a way through this book. Ladies, we are never too old to learn and never too old to change. WE have to pay attention to what we are doing when we find ourselves in the same barnyard over and over. PAY ATTENTION, LADIES! THIS IS THE WAY OUT! SO COME ON OUT, YOU CAN DO IT! LET'S GO!

Nurses Are Good

A nurse has to have a good heart to be a nurse. I feel this has to start from a heart of gold. Now a lot of people go to school to become nurses, and a lot of them go because

1. they have a good heart for the human race;
2. my best friend is a nurse, and she has her own apartment;
3. my mother was a nurse, and I want to be like her;
4. I look real cute in the uniforms;
5. it's easy work and easy money.

No, ladies, if your answer is not number 1, then you will not last being a nurse. You have to have answer number 1 to fit in 2, 3, 4, 5. Without Answer number 1, you will not be able to hang in there long enough to build you a future. And without the answer number 1, I personally don't want you taking care of me as a patient. Because you will be in that position FOR ALL THE WRONG REASONS! And all the wrong reasons are NOT GOOD! And believe me, nurses are good!

They have to study, take tests, and remember what they have studied about. They have to know and remember all the abbreviations all of the other nurses already know, and then the doctors use abbreviations when they dictate and communicate all the time. And what about charting? The nurses have to learn and know how to chart accurately. Then last of all, their patient care is very, very important; so, ladies, if you have seen yourself going into nursing positions, be sure and true to yourself. First, search your heart and then find your true feelings about how you feel about giving other people care.

Then you need to have patience and take your time with the patients. As a good caregiver, ready to face and do the work in any condition to the best of your training that you are asked by your charge nurse to perform. I was once visiting a convalescent hospital, and the nurses that were assigned to that room I was visiting, she did not want to perform any type of nursing skills when asked to do so; she took her purse and walked out (case closed). And this is why I say, if your answer is not from your heart, to help take care of the human race, you will surely be wasting your time and your instructors' time. But, ladies, a GOOD, CARING, CLEAN, WELL-DRESSED, and mentally and physically ready nurse with a strong will is pressing her way to do her nursing duties to the best of her or his ability, I mean TIP-TOP quality work. She or he will be highly favored by GOD because they are givers; GOD loves givers more than takers. And any LOVE-giving nurse can be called nothing but GOOD, so we all have a job to do. GET READY, GET STRONG, and GET BOLD! If you don't have it, FIND IT, TAKE IT BACK, AND KEEP IT!

This is the day and time for boldness. THE TIME FOR THE FULL ARMOR that your Bible talks about! This is the day and time to know where we came from. This is the day and time to know where we are going, and how we are getting there! The road has been PAVED, so don't follow the yellow brick road. FOLLOW THE GODLY BOLD ROAD. HE WILL MAKE SURE WE GET THERE! HEAVEN IS WHERE OUR HEAD IS! UP! (AND THAT'S REAL!)

Doctors Are Special

Ladies, look how we are so wonderfully blessed to have our doctors. I mean to tell you we have them in every color, in every race, and every country, and they are all over just like GOD is. All over the world, we have medical care, rich or poor. Wherever we go, GOD made sure he put the knowledge in them. Making and keeping the human race safe from germs and keeping us feeling better day-by-day. We have our GOD watching over us every minute of the day; he never sleeps, and he makes sure we have doctors around the clock.

When one doctor is asleep, two doctors are on duty, and we know that things are being done about the hurt and the ill people all the time. So we won't take that lightly but with a humble heart and "Thanks." GOD made your doctor and my doctor when they were in their mother's wombs. He gave his wisdom in the womb, and after they were born, he started molding in them all the knowledge of being able to learn what they would need to walk into their destiny and yearning as young children. Whether they knew it or not, they were born to be GOD'S HANDS here on earth. Just think about all the things doctors can do. They know if we are too hot, that something is wrong with us, and they start digging in the pile of hay (IF YOU WILL) to find out why we are hot! Then we have our surgeons who know how and where to cut and take out or replace the problems inside our bodies. And they also know and study everything about our brain; how wonderful is that? And one day soon, with the guidance of GOD'S HANDS, they will come up with the GREAT WEAPON that will send cancer back to the pits of hell where it came from! THEY took all that time in school and college to find out how to make us feel better and live longer. I salute every doctor on this earth, and I know each and every one of them is so special in GOD'S eyes.

They have their own spot in the eyes of GOD. A lot of them have to be our nurse, our crying pillow, our special relying friend, our adviser, and we learn to put our trust in them to pull us through the hot spots, and they keep us from

108

slipping through the cracks, in and out of the hospital. They are away from their families and loved ones most of the time just to take care of us. Doctors give up so much of their personal time here on earth; when we need them, they are there. Seems to me they've put us first and family last when they really don't have to. But the GOD in them and the heart they were born with keeps them caring about you and me!

Some of them go without a meal or put it off until they make sure we are okay! I have seen them take late lunches and wait around for x-rays to come back. I can't help myself; I have to give our doctors their props! Where would we all be if GOD had not called out the doctors we have today? Ladies, we must pay more attention to our blessings that come through our doctors. Believe me, they are from HEAVEN especially made with love, peace, and quietness; that's why they learn like they do. They came from a SPECIAL BATCH! Every one of them individually made, not one is made the same. GOD knew exactly where he wanted them to be placed. So I would like to invent a "Special Appreciation Day" for ALL our wonderful hardworking doctors in this WHOLE world! Everybody should go all out of their way to say "THANK YOU, THANK YOU, THANK YOU!" TO EVERY DOCTOR WE CAN! WE WILL CALL IT LOVE YOUR DOCTOR DAY. THEY ARE SO VERY, VERY SPECIAL!

Let the Good Times Roll

When we *let the good times roll*, why is that saying read to be ugly, nasty, or totally out of control? As females, our good times can roll in a beautiful way; again, our choice is in control. Letting the good times roll does not always mean men and sex. We have been rollin' since we were children. Now we roll on another level; no matter what we do, we can't stop rolling. You can let it roll with our love we have for me, you, and I (better known as me, myself, and I).

Girlfriend, get happy and roll with yourself, get in your car and ride, make sure you get the car washed and waxed inside and out. Go home and get your bubble bath with your music going so you can relax and picture what you are going to do today, so your good time can roll. It's rolling while you are in your bubbles with some soft jazz coming out of the stereo; have you already pictured what you're going to wear? Putting on your clothes, fixing your hair—let's see, fix that hair different today. YOUR HAIR IS YOUR GLORY, remember?

When you roll, you need a new you sometimes. Remember that, girls; we look mo' better, we feel MO' better when our heads are up, and you have to feel good to let the good times roll. If there is no good feeling there in your heart, no good times will roll. BELIEVE THAT! So we have our rolling, don't we, girlfriend? And the good times make you put on the clothes you love to roll in. Now, rolling could mean rollin' to your best friend's house or your mother's house, rolling to the movie, rolling to church, sometimes rolling to work. But rolling to work is not letting the good times roll unless you make work a good time. Some of us do make work a good time, but a lot of us don't know how to do that.

My point is, girlfriend, wherever we are and whatever we are doing, we have the power to push the good time button on. Yes, the good times could mean a good man waiting, but it's time to learn how to let the good times roll more yourself. Start learning how to enjoy yourself! Make your roll so you focus on your happiness. Let the good times roll when you drive your beautiful car that GOD BLESSED YOU WITH. You know, if life has dealt you a lemon, GOD will make lemonade; that's why we don't need to get stressed out. GOD is always on the throne; he sits HIGH AND LOOKS LOW. Girls, relax. GOD's got us, so we need to just roll in the gym and get our metabolism working.

Now we are full of pep, so the good roll is on! GOT THAT! Roll in on some good shopping you have not done for yourself; go for a salad that we won't feel bad about eating. I want to roll in on some good health; how about you girlfriends? We need to take care of our bodies in and out. Roll on being alive and love the bodies we have. If you're reading this book, your body has truly loved you! If we're not liking them much, then let the good times roll and fix them up.

We need to roll in the mirror more than usual if we start looking closer to the woman in the mirror; we see what we don't like, then we can start seeing what we can like about her if she changes the way she has been rolling. Now she can start letting the good times roll as she makes the changes for her good. I'm talking about us. If you are looking in the mirror and you see all the bad things in or on you and you can't imagine any good changes rollin' in, get out of the mirror; you're not ready to roll! We have to start in the mirror, girls. YOUR GOOD TIMES START WITH YOU!

No one else can let the good times roll in you; it's your choice only. Now that we know we're in charge, do something you've never done for yourself. LET'S SEE! Plan a vacation; plan a party with the girls. If you press your way, then you can always get to the beach. How many of us have never taken a roll to the beach? That's one thing you must do. Mother Nature wants you at the beach. You have to be real and go there, you know. It's NOT NICE TO FOOL MOTHER NATURE! And she always likes our presence at the beach. Now that's a real good time to let it roll as women. Put that on your calendar; if you have not been, you need it. You will love it! It's for you, girl, even if you only kick back an hour. And it's up to you if you don't want to wear a swimsuit, shorts or knee-length pants, or a skirt that blows with the ocean (just don't let it blow up). When you walk barefoot, you can let your feet and toes push down in the sand; that's a feeling you will love, and the wind will blow in your hair as the waves hit the shore with a carefree sound. You can look up at the sky, see the clouds, and talk to your best friend.

The beach is a beautiful place to talk to him, especially if you're asking for something special. He's there, girlfriend. I remember another way to let the good times roll was singing the gospel; it was like magic singing in the church choir. We used to go to so many churches and places to sing; we once even went to Texas to have church and sing at this conference. We had our own hotel; my sister and my nieces were there, and my brother-in-law. We had a good time except for the rain. We had brought our new outfits (all packed up) and met the rest of our church members there and got to sing at the church my pastor grew up in.

We had on red-and-white robes; that day was so wonderful and, boy, did we sing for GOD on that rainy day. We forgot about the weather, I'm telling you all. And, girlfriend, we were letting the good times roll. Singing is real comforting for us, so if you don't sing at all, start! YOU need that! Singing is so good for our insides, our hearts, our lungs, our voice box, and our souls, so sing! LISTEN UP, this version of letting the good times roll is messy but so fun. We get with people we love and go in the backyard and have about SIXTY WHIPPED CREAM PIES ready, and DO YOU KNOW WHAT to do with them? YES, you throw them in each other's FACE!

Oh, you want to laugh deep down in your guts, well, this is it! See, the good times roll with nothing but happiness and good fun. Then you get the water hose, and everybody washes each other's faces. Put on dry clothes, have a bite to eat, then kick back! SOUNDS LIKE FUN? Letting good times roll can truly mean a good game of SPOONS! Spoons mean if you have five people playing, you need only four spoons because one person will not get one. You pass cards around clockwise, try to get four of a kind; when you do, don't say anything. Just quietly pick up a spoon. Soon the others will notice and the next thing you know, all the spoons are gone; someone will not get one, so that person is called an S. If he loses again, he is called an S-P; if he does not get a spoon the next time around, that person will be called an S-P-O, and when he spells out the word *spoon*, that person is out of the game.

Then you take out one spoon because only four people will be playing. And, girlfriend, you know who was the champ of spoons? Must I say more? This was one of those games we played when it snowed outside, and it was too cold to go out and you had no choice but to stay in. Well, this is what was rolling, SPOONS! And if we had creamed eggs on toast and Kool-Aid, the good times were really rolling. A good way to roll is to forgive someone who did something wrong to you; FORGIVE and roll on about your life with the good you have inside of you. Stay away from the bad drama. YOU can roll with sharing good thoughts and ideas with others and give them a positive way to roll, pass on the good news, and just let it roll so someone else can pick up some good times down the road; if we all pass on the good in us, it can go on and on and on.

We MUST PASS THE BATON. I know the good times roll when you, or we, shop for music! That's always a good feeling. Music is wonderful, and if you go in a good music store, you can put on earphones and listen to all kind of good music; and if you are with a group of women, everyone has her own taste of music. You can learn what other people are thinking, feeling, and loving through the music they like. I really think my fancy for music expresses me. I love JAZZ, BLUES, COUNTRY ROCK 'n' ROLL, GOSPEL, BROADWAY, CLASSICAL, and I even have a CD I ordered; it's OPERA by MARIAN ANDERSON. Girls, yes, we can let it roll with our choice of music. YOU ROLL THE MUSIC; DON'T LET THE MUSIC ROLL YOU. So come on, all my girlfriends, let's LET THE GOOD TIMES ROLL while we are together in this book. Find you your good time! Find you your safe time, AND LET THE GOOD TIMES ROLL!

It's Your Day

Every day belongs to GOD, and he loves us so much he lets us have a day that we can call ours. Girlfriends, it's your day! What will this saying mean for you? YOUR BIRTHDAY? Well, YES, this is your day; you will count until GOD says count no more. My thought is, girls, EVERY DAY IS YOUR DAY! Every day you wake up is yours; now what you're going to do with your day is like a horse of a different color. I once had a day, my day, I called it my must-have day. It was my wedding day!

I had a beautiful ruffled white wedding gown with a long ruffled train following me down the aisle in a beautiful old church that everyone in Denver knew about (New Hope). As I look back and think today, that's truly what that marriage needed—new hope! But this was my day, and I was not letting anyone or anything cheat me out of it. So I had seven bridesmaids, seven groomsmen, one flower girl, and one ring bearer. My daughter was my maid of honor, and my baby son Jermaine lit the candles with Shirleen's son Jamal, and my oldest son Vinny gave me away.

Then to put the icing on the cake, my second to the oldest sister was a bridesmaid along with my two stepsisters. Then the big bang was my oldest sister and her husband did sing my favorite song, "ALWAYS." I had to talk my second sister into being in the wedding; she finally said yes, and she had her dress made. And it was so beautiful. All the dresses were in my best color in the world—YELLOW—and the girls had on white wide hats and long white gloves. YOU, GIRLS, WERE SO SHARP IN THOSE HATS! The hats spoke out loud as each girl came down to the altar. The groomsmen had on all-white tuxedos with yellow cummerbunds and yellow boutonnieres. My husband had on an all-white with a long tailcoat. He was very handsome that day; even he knew it!

But everyone had something special to do; my husband's baby daughter Tonya sung a song called "Endless Love." I think that's what makes a wedding;

everyone has a part, and they do their best when their turn comes, and that's so special. Just like a wedding cake, it has a piece for everybody, which means the cake has its part to do also. Then our guests bring nice wedding gifts so they have a part in the wedding too.

The organ player plays the wedding march, the pastor directs the wedding vows, and we went through a reception line to talk to all our friends and family that were so nice to come. After that, we took a lot of pictures; then we went over to the reception that was held at the backyard of my husband's sister's house. Oh, before we got there, we left the church in a horse and carriage with me holding a white parasol over our heads as the white horse galloped down the street. We went through downtown Denver, and then my son Vinny picked us up and then we went to his sister's house. The whole wedding was recorded on video so I will always have MY DAY!

It was my day, and that's what I wanted to do with it. And I did. Whatever talent you were blessed with, use it to the fullest. Girlfriend, if you want to sit back and read a book all day, IT'S YOUR DAY! If you want to wash clothes, IT'S YOUR DAY! If you want to sell something not in line with YOUR BUSINESS, get caught, and go to jail, IT'S NOT YOUR DAY! If you choose to watch movies all day, IT'S YOUR DAY! If you want to read your Bible and pray all day long, IT'S YOUR DAY! If you want to clean the house all day, IT'S YOUR DAY! If you want to talk on the phone all day, IT'S YOUR DAY! Remember, ladies, when you choose positive ways to have your day GOD wanted you to have, BELIEVE ME, LADIES, you can make it turn into one of the best days of your time here on earth. BE happy, stay joyful, and keep your heart good and clean, and turn YOUR DAY into something special and wonderful. Your day WILL never be forgotten (IT MUST not), especially not by YOU! So, ladies, HAVE YOUR DAY! BE YOUR DAY! And YOU will know THE FULFILLMENT OF THIS MESSAGE.

Misery, Why Do You Love Company?

Ladies, listen up! Is there always friction when someone has a better position in life than YOU or ME? We are not well with that status. YOU buy a new dress, and I'm MAD, I'M UPSET, I'M QUIET! Now maybe if our hearts were in the right place of LOVE, we all could get blessed with a new dress and more! You know all the guys at work or at the club or at church; I find out, and you change your phone number. Seems you don't think I'm good enough, smart enough, or worthy enough to know or talk to the people you are associated with! Now, ladies, what is wrong here? You may think I don't have many friends (let her find her own friends). Well, she is your friend, so why can't you both have another friend in common? You may think "I WANT MY FRIENDS TO BE AROUND ME MORE!" Ladies, if we show some tender love and care to each other, we can invite each other into our families for outings and a lot of activities.

I have a friend, and she likes to drink liquor every day, and I always had to work. She did not care; I had a house note to pay. I had car payments, which meant I could not stay home from work because I had to drink in the middle of the week but never on a SUNDAY! And she would not come over for one nice drink of wine; she wanted to drink all night! She always made sure she brought you your favorite drink so you would not tell her "NO! Come back another time." She did not have a job; she lived with her mother and father, where the bills were paid whether she worked or not! But I had my own home I bought alone, with three children that love me dearly. I would think to myself, *She has no children, no privacy in her own home, and she could care less if I lost my job, my home, car, or children for that matter!*

And if I lost all I was striving for, I would be just like her—HAVING NOTHING! Why didn't she respect what I was trying to do—keep my home and my job? As her friend (letting her come over and have a drink), she was not at all validating anything I was about! So finally I had to WISEN UP and JUST SAY *NO*! I did not want to be her company any longer. I told her I don't want any company until I had my days off from work! Call ME ON MY DAYS OFF, OK! Well, she stopped calling me at all. And I knew if I were like her (being miserable all the time and drinking every chance I got), she would like me better because we would surely have a lot in common—MISERY. BUT GOD LED ME THROUGH THAT TUNNEL. Sister, IF MY HOUSE IS CLEAN AND NEAT, I LOVE TO SEE YOUR HOUSE CLEAN AND NEAT! And now in this day and time, we might have to help each other through. There is no time for ENVY OR JEALOUSY to be around us at all. LADIES, this is my own thought on the story, and again, we can go back to the time and age WHEN the devil wanted to have the GLORY and the PRAISE, but he was miserable and confused, out of line, and truly out of position. Well, GOD threw him with his spirit of misery and his company that followed him around. OUT OF HEAVEN, Satan (knowing he was in misery) was glad that GOD threw him out with his COMPANY!

They were all thrown out into the ABYSS OF DARKNESS—into nowhere, floating and tumbling in DARKNESS! I think that's how he became the DARKNESS! He got used to it while floating in the DARK space that GOD threw him in. My opinion is, that is why he's called the Prince of DARKNESS or the DARK SPIRIT OR the SPIRIT OF DARKNESS (if you will). HELL is dark because that's where the enemy came from. I didn't say he came from heaven because he wanted his own praise. (That is not a heavenly spirit.) I say he came from DARKNESS because that's where GOD put HIM! SO MISERY LOVES COMPANY, starting with MR. MISERY HIMSELF that didn't have anywhere to live or exist; he was looking at nothing but DARKNESS! And he still is. THE DEVIL! THAT'S THE FIRST MISERY THAT CAME FORTH! So misery loves company. BUT NOW, LADIES, just think if MR. MISERY did not have any company; that means the devil is without his demons, no bad spirits to send out to tempt and bother us. See, he could do more with the demons to run his dirty errands for him.

THAT'S WHY MISERY LOVES COMPANY. Ladies, please know misery without demons means NO spirits are put before us to tempt us to things LIKE STEALING, FIGHTING our FAMILY MEMBERS OR ANYONE, FILTHY WORDS COMING OUT OF OUR MOUTHS, SEX OUT OF WEDLOCK, KILLING (OR EVEN THE THOUGHT OF TAKING ANOTHER PERSON'S LIFE), and ALL THE LARGE AMOUNT OF BACKBITING WE DO TO ONE ANOTHER! THE GANGS WOULD NOT HAVE ANY PULL TO GET OUR CHILDREN TO JOIN THEIR MURDERING GROUPS OF WHAT'S SUPPOSED TO BE HUMAN

BEINGS! NO CRACK DEALERS CAN'T GO TO AND FRO WITH THE TEMPTATION OF ANY KIND OF DOPE. The demons would not be there to tempt us with bad ideas or bad fattening foods; we would not be tempted to pulling bad and dangerous actions on another human being. No temptations on teenagers fighting or killing their parents, and I could go on and on. But without misery having his company, it would be hard for the evil one to get us to do some of these things all by himself. He's a bad spirit, but without the demon spirits to help (with no company), the world would be such a better place. That's why we have to keep the BLESSED HOPE and our FAITH; with that, MISERY can't come close to us. That is the way my heart feels about misery. And REMEMBER, ladies, THE COMPANY, WE SISTERS HAVE TO BE IN WITH EACH OTHER MUST BE A GOOD COMPANY—HELPFUL COMPANY, ENCOURAGING COMPANY, AND MOST OF ALL, LOVING COMPANY! THAT'S WHY, IF MY HOUSE IS CLEAN AND NEAT, I LOVE TO SEE YOUR HOUSE CLEAN AND NEAT TOO! AND, LADIES, WE NEVER HAVE TO BE COMPANY TO MR. MISERY EVER AGAIN. AND THAT'S REAL. THIS IS TRULY THE TIME. LADIES, LET'S DO THIS!

Let's Be Thankful

Rejoice and be glad all up in this day. Your joy is here this morning. Let your soul grab some; we will feel so much better with that JOY ALL DAY LONG than to go through the day with just nothing. Today, make sure you know and anyone around you knows that your day today is more special than yesterday. BECAUSE IT IS! Listen up, ladies. I once had a good friend; everyone called him DOC. He was the well-known DJ in the main city of Denver. I mean he was so good and special about what he did as a DJ that the mayor of Denver would call on him; every time he would have something special that called for music, he would call on DOC. See, DOC knew all kinds of music; just tell him what the occasion is that you are having, and he had music to go with the occasion.

Anyway, the mayor loved DOC and his music. I used to think that was so cute! Well, DOC was well-known and liked all over. He would come around when I gave plays; he would help me put the music in order and make sure the sound was where he wanted it to be. He was about perfection when it came to his music work. He later joined the church where I belong to and no longer played music as a DJ in the nightclubs. He once told me he wanted to use what God gave him; "FOR GOD from now on," and he did. He wanted people in the clubs to know he gave his life and work to GOD. I remember once he was talking to his wife Shirleyfae and me about the people in the clubs had been saying around town that he had died. And he would say, "Yes, I died to the life of being out in the clubs." And I'm a witness that he was very serious about his work for GOD! His work was no joke, and he would make sure you knew it. Ladies, he was so thankful every day, even when he had undergone dialysis to get his blood cleaned; GOD BLESS HIM! He would spend so much time in the bathroom waiting for GOD to let him pass water (if you will, one more time). He would say, "I don't want to ask GOD for things. I only want one blessing. I want to pass water!" That's all he wanted! That was his everyday prayer, every day, every night, day in, day out. All he wanted was to go one more time. And GOD called him home before he ever did. And often when I go to the bathroom, I think about DOC, and I say, *GOD, thank you for allowing me to go one more time!*

We take so many things for granted. They seem to be small things, but we all sometimes expect that we will never have a problem such as that. Now, ladies, you can't imagine going in the bathroom and sit down to pass water and nothing comes out. You have the feeling and the pressure is on your bladder but nothing comes out! Now your brain is telling YOU something's WRONG! Ladies, we have to be more thankful for every LITTLE STEP and every GIANT MOVE we make. Every INHALE, EVERY EXHALE, THE OPENING AND SHUTTING OF OUR EYES, OUR SMELL, OUR TASTE (which I don't have at this moment), THE LITTLE THINGS ARE VERY NECESSARY. Without the little things working, later on, the big things won't count! LADIES, LET'S be more thankful, and let others see that we are. WE can give a good message to others just by letting them see and notice the change of our being thankful for the little things.

Then you will have your door open, and GOD can put your BIG BLESSING in THERE. BECAUSE HE LOVES YOU SOOOOOOOOOOOO MUUUUUUUUUCH!

Forever Mother and Daughter

I'LL ALWAYS LOVE MY MOTHER. SHE'S MY FAVORITE GIRL. I'LL ALWAYS LOVE MY MOTHER. SHE BROUGHT ME IN THIS WORLD

YOU ONLY GET ONE, YOU ONLY GET ONE. What happened to those sayings, ladies? We need to keep her love with us until OUR END! Not her end, our end. She's so special. If it were not for her body, you and I would not know life (if you will). GOD said HONOR her, or he will shorten your days here on earth. To honor her is to LOVE her! I can't cope when I hear on the news, someone killed their mother! Ladies, we are so special as I told you earlier in the book. Nothing on earth can match us. Mother and daughter are forever! So many fun and good times mother and daughter can have especially in this day and time. LET'S SEE! We have shopping, swimming, singing, traveling together, MAKEUP, MAKE DOWN, laughing together, church together, driving cars together (YES, we enjoy a good drive! And picking out cars together is so fun), COOKING together, cleaning together, working out together with your mother (so fun). Even having the flu, with Mom around, you're going to get well fast; she knows how to help make the pain more bearable. That's the power of a mother.

And, ladies, if you have a mother alive that can still ride a bike, go for it. That's a rare opportunity. That's putting in time you will never forget no matter how old you get to be. Please know, ladies, that mothers win BATTLES for her babies; THAT'S POWER FROM GOD he gave her before you were born. And, ladies, you got the same POWER before you had your BABIES. We know when they are hurt; we know when they are choking. We know when they are unusually cross; we know when our children act different. We know when they have done something wrong, and we know when they are happy or unhappy. GOD GAVE MOTHERS A SPECIAL AWARENESS THAT HOOKS ON TO OUR BABIES.

I CALL IT "INVISIBLE AFTER BIRTH" if you will. I can't think of anything else to connect us closer than that! So I have to express this POWER as best as I can. ARE YOU FEELIN' THIS STRENGTH, LADIES ? Mother and daughter are SOFT together. They ARE PINK AND FLUFFY TOGETHER. They are COLOGNE together and BEAUTIFUL, BEAUTIFUL MUSIC TOGETHER. Good music is good for both of you. Then comes the cooking, measuring, tasting, and smelling things, which brings out laughter and jokes on the side. My daughter came the other morning and washed my feet in this antitoxic foot tub. It brought out some different colors in the water. It turned beige, gold, then brown, so I guess I had so many different toxins in me that I never knew about. Then she rubbed them with lotion, so it was a good little time we had together.

The color of the water tells things about you and your body, but I don't think I was supposed to know anything about that, so I just played like I didn't know a thing. That's what mothers are supposed to do sometimes. Ladies, it's not good to know it all! We want our daughters to know and learn all she can about MONEY, JOBS, and PEOPLE in the world. I did always say no one in this world will sit a JOB on your LAP! You must get up, grab your future, and hold on! In this day and time, you have to hold on and hope you get a RIDE! I told my daughter, "As long as you work, you can have anything you want in this world!" Since she's a female, I had to plant that SEED in her heart and in her head because sometimes we LADIES get put on the BACK OF THE BUS (if you will). Mothers, we have to LOVE OUR DAUGHTERS no matter what she's not doing to please us. She has her own way, and you and I have to accept her way, SIMPLE AS THAT! DAUGHTERS are leaving this earth sooner than they should, and I want to stop some of that in any way I can. Some MOTHERS are laying their DAUGHTERS to rest, and that's not the way it's supposed to be. I always feel a broken heart inside me when I think of the Mexican American singer SELENA. Her mother had to see her DAUGHTER DEAD! OH, WHAT A HURT THAT HAS TO BE! SHE IS ALWAYS IN MY PRAYERS. OUR GIRLS ARE SO PRECIOUS TO US. That's why we want them treated like QUEENS! AND THAT'S ALL I HAVE TO SAY ABOUT THAT!

Hidden Talents

Your talents could be your blessings from GOD, so you must not be ashamed to use them (or even get too old to use them). We used to play a game when I was a little girl; it was called SLEEPYHEADS GO BY. Well, ladies, that game can come true! My older sister and I were talking about different hairstyles, and she says she used to love fixing other girls' hair in cute styles and making them feel good and look good; and she said she never got tired, and she had the talent to braid hair. We were saying how women can go and buy hair in any style now in this day. She was always doing office work (she also was a nurse in her younger days). I asked her why she never tried to get her professional status in doing hair.

Her answer was, "I don't know!" She just thought, "I don't know why I never tried to go into doing hair." She really loves hair, and her pastor made a comment and said, "You never see a strand of hair out of place on my sister's hair." She was good at doing hair and had been born with the talent but never thought about making money with her gift, her hidden talent. If you don't step up, you'll miss out on showing your talents. And they'll stay HIDDEN! Even when your blessed to teach or preach, if you're not in the right place at the right time, your God-given talents are still hidden (if you can sew and make pretty dresses and you never speak on it or think about what it is you can and love to do).

Just like we all watch *American Idol.* If those people did not stand in those long lines, the talents they have would never be known; then they might grow old and then think they were almost singers once. BUT LADIES, my point is if you sing, dance, draw art, make pretty hairstyles, pray good, cook good, act on stage good, or whatever you know you can do and you keep it under your belt, it could make you very happy. This could be your ultimate stage of your life, and you need to step forward. Don't be afraid of your destiny! This could be it; if you don't try, you will never know. I say take a chance, step out, and test the waters. We have a lot of our favorite stars in Hollywood. What if a lot of them thought like "I can't," "No one will like me," "I was not born with any talent," "Everything I do is wrong," "I don't know what to say," or "I don't want anyone looking at me"? Ladies, put away all the REASONS and walk the walk. This is our fulfillment of what we were put here to be or do!

This is part of letting the good times roll. Let it start rolling with your DREAMS, YOUR TIME IN LIFE, YOUR NERVE, YOUR PRIDE, and YOUR WOMANHOOD; you are so special, ladies. Don't play Sleepyheads Go By. DON'T SIT ON YOUR HAPPINESS ANYMORE! GET UP! LET'S GET STARTED. And most of you, ladies, should move on your talent while you are young. You can do more with your youth on your side. So find the rest of your good intentions here on earth; a lot of your findings are getting you in line to get your crown whenever the promised land is ready for you. You are working on it now! SAY WHAT THE BOY SCOUTS SAY—BE PREPARED! That is what we all should be doing, believe that! But putting that on another shelf, you can finally make yourself happy, and the MYSTERY word for this BOOK is ME. Now you can find all the ways you can use that MYSTERY word for your own good!

I used to want to play an instrument, but I never took the time out to learn. I think I have a talent for music and rhythm, so I missed out on some good fun and happiness; I kept it HIDDEN. So if you can play the piano or any other musical instrument, please do so. Don't sit on it and think forever. Walk into the world of music; there's MAGIC in there for you! Don't let it pass you by; I can't stress that enough! And playing music for other people can make them happy also; that's why we buy CDs, tapes, and such to BE HAPPY! OUR TROOPS ARE HAPPY WHEN WE SEND THEM MUSIC. Without music, our TROOPS would BE so SAD! Music makes you clean up good too! HOUSEWORK LOVES MUSIC ALSO! OH, and, LADIES, I have already written to you about the happiness of our DANCE. We need that—DANCE; GET YOU ONE! I always wanted to dance the TANGO, but so far, I haven't and I won't give up the dream. I'm KEEPING the DREAM ALIVE!

Play On

Ladies, by this time in life, we know the talk is that there's a shortage of men. And since there is, why must feelings get hurt and hearts be broken? When we look at a broken heart, it is usually nine out of ten! The broken heart of a woman, now I know men have hearts and they get broken just like a woman's heart. The difference is when a man's heart is broken, it is fixed very quickly by having another woman out to dinner and a drink then usually to BED, whether it be at home or a HOTEL, MOTEL, or HOLIDAY INN. So a man is on his job getting rid of the HURT of losing his woman, wife, or friend (as he calls it!). LADIES, I noticed when a man has a wife (he could be a preacher or an auto worker) and his wife gets sick, some men don't wait until she dies (unless he has a good insurance policy). When the wife dies, LO AND BEHOLD, he has another woman in bed without letting the wife even get the grave cold for a week or a month before he has another woman in his arms! Isn't his wife worth MOURNING a week? You can forget a year of mourning for his precious wife of thirty or forty years. He usually has another woman in her bed and her beautiful home before she has been in the ground a week! See, LADIES, the thing I hate so much (I don't know about you!) is that we are so easily and quickly replaced, especially when we die! We can't do a drive-by to let him know we're still around (SMILE). Before you can say, "HEY! She has our FURS, DIAMONDS, SATIN SHEETS, and CAR for herself" because he's so glad not to be in there alone, he will give her anything we had just to keep her, even if he's not in love! Now if some men know she's sick and not going to be around long, he's usually already making plans with another woman. LADIES, I'm not saying he should not have another woman. There are so many of our men who do this whether we are dead or alive, and that just makes me SICK! LISTEN UP, LADIES. Now I need to turn the tables—he's sick and maybe going to leave this earth and leave you, me, or us here to carry on. We, ladies, will cry, moan, look at his pictures, smell his clothes, look at his car (and the way he left it, where he left it), keep his ring or watch, play his music, get a glass of wine and cry, and keep talking about something he said or did (as long as we can or as long as someone else will listen to our memory of him). That's some of our ways, as wives, we want to hold on to anything he's left here so we can have a little more of him a little longer.

WHY do some of us feel GUILTY even if we think about being with another man? We actually get mad at ourselves for wanting to be with another man! Well, our man is gone (per se), so why can't we? Why don't we put a man on his sheets or in his car and bring out his clothes and see if our new man can fit any of them if he wants too? (Some of us can do this.) BUT, LADIES, we are just not made with such hard hearts! WE TREASURE the thirty or forty YEARS we had with our man, and those years can't ever be touched by anyone; we won't allow IT! That's the way most of us, ladies, are. I personally would like all of us to be REMEMBERED, if we have to go, and MOURNED a little longer. I need and wish our men could show the world we were a special part of their lives and not just put us on the shelf (if you will). Some of us BROUGHT his CHILDREN IN THIS WORLD, so why do they want to forget us so quickly? IT'S JUST NOT FAIR!

I saw this done to so many of my dear friends and my poor mother that bore seven children with pain from her body for two no-good men, and it hurt me! THEY were good women! And, ladies, if a DIVORCE is in play, he will really have her there before you can blink ten times. IF a DIVORCED woman has a man before her husband has a woman, I tip my hat to you because usually he's always playing ahead. So, LADIES, we need to get HUNGRY for our hearts to be unbroken every time we SLIP and let our GUARDS DOWN. Some of us don't SLIP; we walk around in our homes, in our marriages, in our SPACE with no GUARD UP AT ALL! Ladies, whatever the case, we have earned the RIGHT with our men to BE LOVED and TREASURED more than he can think about being LONELY. And if he chooses to PLAY with our "BROKEN HEARTS" and our "MEMORIES," then PLEASE KNOW, LADIES, GOD SITS HIGH AND LOOKS LOW and tells us, LADIES, "THIS IS A GOD JOB. LET ME HANDLE IT!"

Pass It On

Ladies, as women and adults, we must always be aware and think about what a good message we are giving and leaving behind us. As a good human being, we must take the baton and pass it on so the next person or generation will know a path to take and not be left out or sideswiped on making a good or wise decision. The thing that gets me thinking is when we have bad advice or bad taste in picking our men. BAD habits such as drinking liquor all our young lives, being on drugs, bad eating habits, or gaining weight (like our ancestors or our parents did), then we have a no working record like our parents might have had.

So we don't like to have any kind of job. Since I was a child, we did not have any example showing us we had to work. And we surely don't want to leave out higher education. (YOU always hear no one in my family went to college! Why should I?) Not even thinking that is the reason we should want to go, so we can leave something good to pass on. Fathers sometimes leave a long jail record and pass it on to their sons and daughters. How can a long rap sheet in the police department be a good baton to pass on? Prison should not be passed on; ways to stay out of prison should be passed on. WATCH THAT, fathers! To the young people in and out of our families, you need a village to show you there is something else to do in this life so that message can be passed on and on and on. This is the legacy and birthright for all our children! So pass on those smart and helpful ways, and means that need to be grabbed by all the hungry generations.

There will be generations waiting in line for a way to stay afloat in this world. I have seen over and over that; it is real easy and natural for our family members and parents to pass on poverty. Why, I'm allergic to poverty! I always had a breakout of rash when I was a child. Now I know why! I was allergic to poverty, and no one did anything about that! Every time poverty would come near me, I would break out in a sweat, get nervous, and really switch to being a very unhappy person to be around. I can't take the reactions to poverty, so I don't want to leave that word unconquered and pass it on. It's not right, it's not fair; someone has to make things change. So if it has to start with me, then I'm here to set a different path for anyone in my family and my village. Now, LADIES, in my view of life, I am saying to our young loved ones, "Go to school, get your skills, learn well, and learn all you can about HOW you will make your money." When you MAKE your money, no one can take it. When you steal your money, the police can take it 'cause it was not yours to start with! No one, no one can manage your money unless you choose for them to.

But, ladies, we all must learn to save and put our money to good use; make sure you can see your money. While at home, take a LOOK around at WHY you GO to WORK! And while at work, you need to know and see why you get up in the morning no matter what the weather is, YOU go to work each day! So if you have a car you purchased with your work money or you brought yourself a new house, television, clothes, or planning a vacation, well, you know where your money is! And that is why you get up every morning and go to work. Now I wanted to pass that on to anyone who thinks he or she works for nothing! Ladies, take your next step forward because we need to pass on love, and I know we can pass on knowledge. Then we need to pass on understanding because if you don't understand what is coming your way, then you won't be able to GRAB it! So understanding things in life is very, very important. Then comes a chance to pass on some courage. Isn't this good, ladies? And I surely want to pass on the word *STRENGTH* to everyone. You will need your strength! And then, ladies, we have to pass on determination (I need that word so much for me right now!). And I would like to pass on joy, happiness, and peace. (We need those words all year long, not just every Christmas!) I need to pass on hearing—hearing the word of God; we can't leave that out! I want to pass on my visions, my voice, and my thoughts. If I had my way, I would pass on my strength from colors, my joy from acting, my seriousness of love, and most of all, I would like to pass on the peace I have in my SOLITUDE because that is the time I find that I know me.

Ladies, you may think you know yourself in a crowd or in public places. I want to pass on a little SOLITUDE to you too so you will find you for yourself. You will certainly find you're not such a doubtful you after all. So, ladies, let's go forth with goodness from now on. Go forward and find what good out of your life that you know you should and can pass on. As part of a good village, I think cooking and baking would be a good rate to pass on as long as our offspring does not overdo it. So we definitely need that word—*discipline*—to be on the pass-on list. Having good office skills should be passed on. I love decorating, so I want to pass it on; it's good and fun, and fun always has to be passed on.

Being married, having a beautiful wedding and a good working husband, and having children that can be taken care of physically and financially should be passed on because so many of us don't know the direction of being good dependable parents. So anyone that has done a good job with that needs to pass it on to the village. My mother tried, but she could have done a better job if the BATON was passed on; she could have learned and done a better job of mothering all seven children and getting more REST for herself. I could have been different! Then I could have been a better mother for my little babies that I love so very, very much! Seems like if my mother had been shown how to handle seven children or was given some advice about how to make things work better with her work schedule, she would have gotten more REST and less STRESS at home. (That's what I thought!)

I know when you have that many children, you have to have SOME ORDER and a program to follow daily. That is the only way the mother that just had eight babies is ever going to ever be alone with the babies as they grow; she's gotta have some ORDER. Without that ORDER, raising that many children on her own will be a disaster for the children and herself. Ladies, moving on, good dancing has to be passed on too because we need the good time and especially since our country is having a hard time right now. Another important message to pass on—FAMILY EATING AT THE DINNER TABLE TOGETHER every night, or as much as possible, because that's when family communication falls in (and we all need that time), and it brings closeness. And a family with closeness is happy and needs to be passed on. We all know—a family that prays together stays together. And in this day and time of life, the BATON has to be passed on, HAND TO HAND. So, ladies, sit down and ask yourself, "What will or can I pull good from my life, from my inner self, to put in another's hand so they too can PASS IT ON!"

TRUE YOU

Ladies, listen up, we can fool others around us and let them see and think we are good, sweet, and nice. I'm learning more and more every day that as ladies, our hearts have to be true: first, true to yourself, then true to me, and then true to them. Our true love and feelings for others in this world has got to be in our hearts; if I, as a woman, had no meekness in my life or my heart, then nothing is real about what I've been saying in this book. This book is out of my heart and out of the good and hurt feelings from my heart. But I choose to share my feelings that are in and had been in my heart—good, bad, or fun with you personally. When you read this book, I am just sitting down, talking with you—YOU AND ME, YOU AND I, and of course, with God in the midst because in his word, he said he is. "Where two or three are joined together in my name, there am I in the midst" (MATTHEW 18:18-20). As my GOD and THE LOVE OF MY LIFE, HE IS MY appetizer AND MY dessert OF EACH DAY! WHO really is the true you? Do you love HER? Do you like who she is? Or would you rather not know her? ARE you the true you? If not, can you change to be the true you that you really want to be To BE THE TRUE YOU? We ask the question, how can I change her? Answer: start to think differently, talk differently, and speak good to her! WILL IT COST MONEY? HOW MUCH? Yes, it will take some money. We need a new look to go along with the new heart and the new way of thinking, so we will need a new look in the mirror. We have to change the way we eat; some of us, ladies, do. I know I do! SO, yes, it will cost a little extra to eat and think different. We will be a different person in and out of our bodies. Some might need a new hair look, so we can identify the true you when you see her.

That's only the outside of you you're going to look at. Now, ladies, the real question is when and how will we see the woman inside. How can the lady inside change? This means young ladies, in-their-prime, and old ladies. Whatever our age is, it's not real important, but the earlier we are changed from our old ways, the less we need to fix it as we grow older. GOT THAT? No woman is born perfect at this age and time in this world. So if you are young and have a good-patterned disciplined woman in your midst, watch her closely and listen to her advice. Look at her sweetness, hear her choice of words, and watch all her steps as she walks forward in her own life. This is a good direction we need to go. Is she good with money choices? If she is, she's never broke and can always go in her purse and GIVE! Then watch how she runs her house and what bills she pays and when she pays them. How she shops for her family is a good pointer to having money left in our purses.

And, ladies, if she talks to GOD out loud, please pay attention. She is giving you all the keys to peace of mind early in your life. Then when you reach what is called your PRIME age in life, you are prepared for the main BATTLES in life. You can press on to grow old GRACEFULLY, just LIGHT as a FEATHER with less worry, less pain, and less bills; everything should be very light by the time you get old. All these should be over or at least quiet and safe. That's why we have to get the cookbook out. Now the recipe has to be right so our meal will come out light (if you will) AND WELL DONE! Then we pray that the TRUE YOU will love the new way she LOOKS, SPEAKS, AND WALKS through a new life you, me, and I have to have from this day forward. LADIES, WE WOULD NOT HAVE IT ANY OTHER WAY!

CORN

The word *corn* let me know that I am and you are, ladies, just as special as any other woman of high status. We are all the same in the eyes of God. God will not say because I or you are not rich (having a big fancy house or not), he does not care for us; less than he cares and loves the president, his wife, or Mother Teresa. We are just as special. Ladies, as I look back in my childhood days, I never felt like I was important or popular in school 'cause I had the best clothes or the most lunch money every day because I didn't! But I know I always had my own mind, and to me, my thoughts were important, and they still are, and I did and do count in this world!

And, ladies, one day, I was about nine years old, and we lived in a corner terrace; it was like a two-bedroom apartment, and there were seven children and two adults, one was you know who—Mr. Friday Night Special. There were about four main corners over in that area, and all the families were black. My friend and her parents lived on one corner. Anyway, on the next corner of Gilpin Street, the other Barbara, Ann, and her family lived. They were pretty well-to-do; they, as children and teenagers, did not want for much. Their mother was a nurse, and their father—he was a very nice person. Back then you didn't have to lock your doors every second. Anyway, Mr. Williams had a filling station on that corner also, and he would sometimes give me a free pop when it was real hot outside. Her little sister Sandra was the cutest laughing girl I knew; she would make things funny!

WE lost her two years ago. Then on the other corner of Gilpin were the EDWARDS family, who I loved very much; that was my favorite place to spend the night! Vanetta was a good friend to me; they were very well-to-do as a black family in those days. Her dad would always come home late at night. I mean after 2:00 in the morning with the best barbeque hamburgers I've ever tasted! To this very day, I've never had one to top it! I lost Vanetta over twelve years ago, but I love her still! Anyway I was sitting in our little backyard (if you want to call it that), and I was so hungry that day my mother was at work as usual, so it was "fend for yourself." With a family of seven children, that wasn't going to be much believe ME!

So I was sitting on the back porch; I was so hungry (never had a weight problem) 'cause there was not much food buying going on in that so-called house! The only thing I could find in the kitchen was some popcorn, and there was nothing there to cook, only a half bag of popcorn seeds! The bad part is there was no oil or any kind of grease to pop it with. I don't even think there was any hair grease (if you will), so I could not pop anything! So I just took the bag of popcorn outside on the back porch and put a couple of seeds in my mouth! That was not the taste! I could not even bite one! I just sat there with them in my hand and rolled the seeds back and forth in each hand.

Then I thought to myself, *I can't eat it. This is a seed.* Then my mind said, "YOU PLANT SEEDS." So I looked at the little bit of dirt in the small little square yard, about as big as a big screen TV (if you will). So I got up, went to the kitchen, got a spoon, ran out the back door like I was hypnotized, and I started DIGGING. I made rows of holes; then I put the popcorn seeds in all the rows of holes I dug! I must have planted quite a bit because as I started to water them every day, several green leaves started to come up. So I started to water them every time I woke up to see if there would be more and bigger green leaves. And each day, it seemed like there were MORE AND MORE AND MORE; THEY WERE TALLER AND TALLER AND TALLER! I loved the BIG BEAUTIFUL LEAVES; they made that yard look big, BEAUTIFUL, AND IMPORTANT! And I felt so special! Now I know why! God was with me. That's how I felt anyway! So I was watering them, and Mr. Friday Night Special caught me bringing water from the house in a jar, and he said, "What the hell you doing with that water you keep spilling on the floor!" I looked down, and I was spilling water, but I had to water the corn; I was only nine years old! So while he was watching me clean up the water off the floor, he followed me out to the backyard, watching me give the corn water; he said, "Why did you put this S—T out here anyway?" SO a strange man came to the yard, and he asked if the "CORN ON THE COB" was for SALE.

So Mr. Friday Night Special said to him, "NO. NOT RIGHT NOW!" The next thing I knew, he was watering the corn with this green hose! He went and bought a new hose to water the corn 'cause we surely did not have any grass! Everyone on the bus that stopped to let people off would look with amazement! You could hear people say, "Wow! Look at that cornfield in the middle of the city!" And a lot of people wanted to buy some, well, we can end this story! Guess who sold the corn on the COB? But, ladies, I look at that corn differently now; it was not who sold it. I see how GOD gave me a spirit of harvest TO TAKE AWAY MY HUNGER!

NIBBLE AND DEVOUR

Ladies, sometimes we want to say, "Men, don't nibble on us so much! With all of your mistreatments, you seem like you don't know how to treat some of us women." A lot of them start nibbling from the first day of "I DO." They start counting on what they will get and what they can get no matter what it is. I pray to God, "LET OUR MEN, ALL MEN, FOCUS ON WHAT THEY CAN GIVE HIS LADY TODAY." Some of our men do think as such. Ladies, there are so many that don't even think near that thought. Then I pray the prayer, "God, if YOU can't show them the way, THEN PLEASE FORGIVE THEM FOR BEING SO LOST." Ladies, keep praying for them no matter what!

Give them a little HINT. A girl needs her back washed sometimes without asking all the time. A GIRL needs her feet rubbed and lotioned. Ladies, we need them to nibble on a whole new purpose of "I LOVE YOU." All of them should know, these things will make it better for them when they show extra TLC! Oh, and when they do, ladies, if they do show us more TLC, don't sit there and act like it's not a big deal. You might make it bad for the rest of us, you feel me on this, ladies? Let him know that you love the good talk and the great treatments. So this can, maybe, get "PASSED ON." Oh yes, ladies, we know he can get another love (as they call it), but how much love is that? And by the time we see what love he chooses over us, WE REALLY KNOW WE DIDN'T BELONG THERE IN THE FIRST PLACE! Some people I know like to be ugly, stinky, and drunk or drugged up. Well, they need someone too. I feel they need and deserve the same type of woman they are! My view is they truly don't need or deserve a DECENT and SMELLING-LIKE-ROSES and GARDENIA-WEARING WOMAN!

That is my thought, ladies. We all fill the same for each other, but we don't and won't have the same decision at the end of all the pain and suffering; the "going in," the "going outs," the "feeling so sorry for them"—most of us still care! But, ladies, if they don't know what to do with a cotton ball, most are too used to having toothpicks made of wood, so it's so hard to change or accept that in this day! I'm with you whatever you think you can still handle. But, ladies, if your safety or your health is not where you want it to be, then we (yes, we are still together) need to make another and a BETTER CHOICE! WE CAN DO THIS! WE'RE TOGETHER! All we have to keep saying to ourselves and each other is YOU CAN LET him nibble on your love and life, but he must not devour. WHEN IT'S DEVOURED, it's ALL GONE, LADIES. YOU CAN'T GET IT BACK!

HIDDEN CAMERA

Ladies, we all know what's done in the dark will always come to the light. See, GOD sits high and looks low; he looks low to us through what's known as a hidden camera because what you do down here, God see's you! Yes, those that are watching and waiting to touch our children will and can go to jail or worse. And just because God is watching those types of people, they will never get away no matter how slick and cunning they may think they are. No one passes through without being seen. God's eyes are "hidden cameras." Ladies and our young women, we have to be on guard and aware at all times when it comes to our babies and our grandbabies. There are men and women out there that like to touch children, and some animals will mess with our little babies.

Some of our young mothers are just not aware like the older mothers. YOUNG MOTHERS, LISTEN UP! A lot of times you have to pay more attention to who you have your babies around. I'm not saying stay away from your friends, but stay on your guard! Some of you let your babies lie in the comfort of any kind of NICE man you think you know, but some will pretend to like you and your baby just to get your baby alone.

While you're shopping, washing, or just even cooking dinner, he will be right under your nose, messing or fondling your baby's private parts. Ladies, we must warn and teach our young mothers (who love sex more than their babies) to wake up and protect your little babies and your toddlers. They are depending on you to keep them safe! And, ladies, I'm speaking on this because I have seen and I feel we, as women, need to teach our young adult mothers, and we have so many young mothers today that just have a baby. They are not aware that this is not a doll; they can't put him or her back in the box and pull it out when they want to play MOMMY!

They have to be led to understand this baby cannot eat or keep itself clean. They can't tell you they are sick ("MOMMY, I HAVE A FEVER") or tell you to change its Pampers when they are wet! Ladies, some of our young mothers don't think to check the baby; if she has changed the baby once, she might not check the baby until four or five hours later. It's sad but it's true! And for some of the young mothers, they just don't think. "I need to pack my baby a good diaper bag if I'm going to be gone all day with my baby," "I need extra milk, extra wipes, and Pampers," "Oh, and I need a change of clothes for my baby, it might be getting cold before I get back home," and "I need to bring some pajamas too so my baby will be clean, dry, and fed and warm enough to not get cold then I can have a better time too because my baby is well taken care of." Ladies, that is sort of how we have to get our younger mother to think and talk. And they need to know they have to be the hidden camera and watch their babies when the men are around. And more so when he's a stray man; we just can't trust them! When I say "hidden camera," I mean our EYES, OUR FEELINGS, AND OUR COMMON SENSE! We must teach our girls to be geared up and always ready for war! They must know what the WHOLE ARMOR OF GOD IS and know when and how to wear the ARMOR. This armor is part of the hidden camera. The enemy can't see THE ARMOR until we start using it on his BIG HEAD! Ladies, let's teach our young ladies and our young adults how to stay focused and how not to let their guard down, open the fence, and let the enemy and his evilness near our babies or our children. We must not let him come in to just DEVOUR our loved ones, our children, and our babies! This part of this book is to help all our sisters—RED, YELLOW, PINK, GREEN, WHITE, OR BLACK—to be ready and know that God has a hidden camera on every minute, every second, and every hour, DAY AND NIGHT! NO more killing and raping our children! We must take a STAND as a strong VILLAGE IN EVERY CITY, EVERY STATE, and EVERY TOWN! The VILLAGE HAS TO BE READY, AND WE ARE! SO I'M SERVING NOTICE to all the demons that are in this world that attack our babies and our children who skip around not knowing they are being preyed on.

Well, the hidden camera is on, and they will fall down in their own mud because that's what they are anyway, nasty mud from hell! Ladies, we are READY to FIGHT for our LOVED ONES that can't help themselves. AS ladies, we will speak for them from now on through our hidden camera that still and always will SIT HIGH AND LOOK LOW. LADIES, WE HAVE OUR ARMOR ON, AND WE ARE READY! LET'S STAND TOGETHER AND MAKE THAT POWERFUL FIST. WE ARE EQUIPPED NOW. WE CAN WIN!

RESOLVED

Ladies, some of us were never allowed as children to have an opinion at home, sometimes at school, and in my house, no ideas were listened to; truly my opinion about something was not to be heard. The saying is "Children are to be seen and not heard." But now in this new generation, a child's opinion is heard and considered important. I was just thinking about when we were children. (I go there a lot, putting two and two together; in other words, connecting the dots. My mind always goes there.)

Anyway, back then if you were of the black race, you were not allowed to move past York Street. Our parents went along with this instruction. Then I saw on television how they are teaching our children in grade school to eat more veggies and like it; then some children did like it. Now when I was in grade school, I had green beans at school, but I never remembered eating green beans, carrots, cucumbers, squash, or any veggie like that! I had tomato and lettuce, and onion sometimes, but never was I told it was good for our bodies. No one ever said what was good for us either. I never heard anyone say that at home or at school. I know at home I never heard of a pork chop or a steak until I got older or went over to one of my friends houses to eat dinner. Our little house had only luncheon meat and chicken on the menu! Oh yeah, pork cutlets and french fries sometimes. Now I don't call that eating healthy, do you, ladies?

My point here, ladies, is, now I can, as a woman, see and listen to what is healthy and good for me to eat and be able to resolve my childhood dysfunctional eating habits that have me out of control and redevelop a new way to shop. Now some of us, ladies, take longer to pick this up than others. But I say better late than never! So for some of us, resolving some childhood problems may start from the kitchen table, and some resolving problems end up being solved in a jail cell.

Some of us as little girls have to carry around with us the memories of being touched by men in the wrong places, and it might even be by your cousin, your stepfather, your uncle, or even your own blood father, and then told not to tell. And a lot of girls did not tell but wanted to so bad! I'm saying this, ladies, to let us know it's not too late to tell! If you were bothered by some grown-up and touched in a ungodly way, it's not too late to TELL. Well, if that monster has already died, you can say to your heart and soul, "RESOLVED." Ladies, usually when someone has been bothered and touched on their private parts (I call it our little pancakes), the enemy wants to tempt you, I, or we, to bother some other little person. I know I did listen to a doctor say that usually when a child has been touched or bothered, he or she is likely to do that act to someone else; that came from a mental medical point of view! Ladies, the devil comes to steal, kill, and destroy! So you can't let him hide! You can't let him hide! We have to let the village know there is a mental person around that does what the devil says and touches little children! He has to be EXPOSED; No more whispering; SAY IT LOUD AND CLEAR—"SOMEONE HAS BEEN TOUCHING ME!" We, ladies, have to let our children (and our grandchildren) know that is wrong! They have to be taught to run and then to tell everybody that looks like a grown person. Don't be afraid to TELL! This is happening more and more in our world and society. Ladies, that's what we must teach in our homes, in our churches, in our schools, in our parks and swimming pool areas, and in every spot that the devil will think he is not being watched. We must help RESOLVE this problem and SPEAK OUT! And teach our MOMS and DADS, AUNTS and UNCLES, GRANDPARENTS, TEACHERS, and PREACHERS to SPEAK OUT and know they are helping this WORLD RESOLVE one BIG UGLY PROBLEM! Ladies, we must teach the word everywhere we go! I say teach the WORD! TELL!

Author's Bio

I was born in Denver, Colorado at the university hospital and I lived here most of my life. I moved to California for a short while but there's no place like home. I'm the mother of a beautiful daughter and two handsome sons. I have always loved being around people, I can truly say I'm a people-person. I love surprising people and making them happy. I spent most of my school life singing and singing in churches as well. I write and direct live play performances. I have my own personal relationship with God, and I keep that going daily. My motto is PRESS ON. I love laughter and colors. I will always be a servant for God and I will always PRESS ON.

N. M.

PHOTO GALLERY

Four Generations

My Grandmother Alice

Her Daughter, my mother, Aline

Me and my daughter, Katrina

Me and Barbara in the Pacific Ocean

The Three Sisters

Grandsons and Me

CFL Drama Ministry "Cast"

My Family

Dad

Niece

Brothers

Cousin

Niece

Sis

Niece

Good Times Rollin'

New Year and My Birthday Celebration

Male Generation

My Star

CHURCH

Cousins

My Dear Friends

♥ My Day ♥

All Us Sisters

Made in the USA
Las Vegas, NV
21 February 2022